The Life Journey of Mema

PRUE KOCKLER

Largo, Maryland

Copyright © 2021 Prue Kockler

All rights reserved under the international copyright law. No part of this book may be reproduced or transmitted in any form or by any means, electronic or mechanical, including photocopying, recording, or by any information storage and retrieval system, without the express, written permission of the author or the publisher. The exception is reviewers, who may quote brief passages in a review.

Christian Living Books, Inc.
P. O. Box 7584
Largo, MD 20792
christianlivingbooks.com
We bring your dreams to fruition.

ISBN 9781562295134

Unless otherwise marked, all Scripture quotations are taken from the King James Version of the Bible. Scripture quotations marked (NKJV) are taken from the New King James Version®. Copyright © 1982 by Thomas Nelson. Used by permission. All rights reserved. Scripture quotations marked (GW) are taken from the God's Word® translation. Copyright © 1995 by God's Word to the Nations. Used by permission of Baker Publishing Group. All rights reserved.

The Life Journey of Mema

Contents

Introduction VII
CHAPTER 1: Humble Beginnings 1
CHAPTER 2: We Became Farmers 7
CHAPTER 3: Evening Star 17
CHAPTER 4: Cotton and Peanuts 27
CHAPTER 5: An Abrupt End 35
CHAPTER 6: The Love of My Life 59
CHAPTER 7: Making a Family 65
CHAPTER 8: Time for Another Plan 85
CHAPTER 9: Back to Where We Started 97
CHAPTER 10: Venture Adventures 117
CHAPTER 11: Our Precious Grandchildren 137
CHAPTER 12: My Parents 145
CHAPTER 13: Wisdom Learned Along the Way 157
CHAPTER 14: Small Glimpses of Memorable Moments .. 167
CHAPTER 15: Those Who Came Before 175

Introduction

I was in a Bible study about Israelites straying into idol worship. When I realized these Israelites were 1st and 2nd generation descendants of the same people for whom God had parted the Red Sea to allow the Israelite's escape from Egypt, I was horrified. I said, "How could the children and grandchildren of the people who saw the miracles of God that enabled them to leave Egypt start worshiping little statues instead of their God of miracles? Did they not know? Did their forefathers not tell them?" All of a sudden, I felt like the roof had fallen on my head! I have not told all my grandchildren about the miracles God has done for me. I have thought about this every day since that day.

Some in the family have told me that my family will probably not even be willing to read this. My answer to that is that God has put on my heart to do this. So, I will do this. Who reads it is not up to me. I would love to read about my grandmother's life written by her. Maybe someday a great grandchild may read this.

A side benefit is that as I continue to age, my mind may not be able to recall my life. I have had a wonderful life and hope to enjoy my memories as I age. If I cannot remember my wonderful life, I will read these writings and enjoy!

Precious memories, unseen angels
Sent from somewhere to my soul

How they linger, ever near me
And the sacred past unfolds.

Precious memories how they linger
How they ever flood my soul
In the stillness of the midnight
Precious sacred scenes unfold.

It is not possible to fully understand the meaning of these miracles in my life without some of my life story. My purpose is not to write the great American novel. It has been a very long time since I studied sentence structure or verb tenses or placement of commas. I know we loved commas more when I was in school than they are loved today. I don't even remember what a dangling participle is, so I am sure that I will dangle plenty of them. There will be plenty of misspelled words. Please spread a little grace and mercy upon these writings and don't bother pointing the mistakes out.

This is all done out of love for my family and the love of my God. I did not always recognize God's hand on circumstances at the time it was happening. Sometimes it takes looking back to see God's hand at work. As I have aged, I have more time to look back, and it is with wiser eyes that I do look back.

Now I will share.

CHAPTER 1

Humble Beginnings

January 1943 was one of the coldest in history in Oklahoma. I was born on January 10, 1943. My dad was at bootcamp preparing to go to war when I was born. His first allotment check from the Coast Guard was not on time. The government was late – can you imagine that? My mother did not have the $7.00 to pay the Okmulgee hospital. They almost did not admit her. She mailed the $7.00 to the hospital when she got the first check.

My mother's father was very dark with coal black hair. He came the next day to pick up my mother and myself to go to Nuyaka to his and Grandma Lanny Belle's farm. Ike (my grandfather) told the nurse that she brought the wrong baby to them. The only other baby in the hospital nursery was a little Indian baby with black hair. My mother had black hair like Grandpa, and yet there I was in my mother's arms, pale and pink with very blond hair.

Mother set her glass of water beside her bed and it froze solid the first night we were at my grandparent's home. The only heat in the old farmhouse was from a pot belly stove in the living room. My grandmother would wash my diapers each day with water from the well that was heated on the wood cooking stove in the kitchen. She used a rub board to wash the diapers. The diapers would freeze before she finished hanging them on the clothesline outside.

My mother gave me my baby book a few years before she died. The interesting thing I read in the baby book was a list of visitors. My dad's two sisters-in-law from Morris came to visit and meet me with gifts. This might sound normal as we all do this today to welcome a new baby into the family. These two aunts came in a big farm truck with no heat in freezing temperatures over unpaved, wet, snowy, dirt roads for some distance.

When I read that it made me love them more than ever. Isn't it wonderful how God's family plan gives us extended family? A child can never have too many people who love them.

Grandma and Grandpa Loyd's farmhouse at Nuyaka, Oklahoma.

Grandma and Grandpa Loyd taken on their 50th wedding anniversary in 1950.

FROM FARM TO OCEAN

When I was six weeks old my mother and I started the bus ride to Palm Beach, Florida. This is where my father was stationed after boot camp. All the Coast Guard men would ride their horses along the coast 24 hours a day looking for enemy ships and submarines. He would have one night a week to come and stay with us. Mother said sometimes we would meet him with a lunch packed and visit with him during his lunch break.

My mother and me in Florida.

Me in Florida in 1944

FROM OCEAN BACK TO LAND

I was a little over a year when my dad was deployed to a tanker ship. He sailed oceans and seas to refuel warships. After leaving my dad, Mother and I rode the bus to Chattanooga, Tennessee. Mother's sister and husband lived there. They were my Aunt Buck and Uncle Levi. Aunt Buck worked days in a sock mill. Mother got a job at the same mill working nights.

Aunt Buck watched over me while Mother worked nights. Mother was born up in the mountains above Chattanooga in Alabama. Mother's family moved to Okmulgee, Oklahoma from Alabama when she was five years old. My mother was the next to youngest of nine children. At that time, the three oldest children were grown. Two of her sisters ended up living back close to where they had grown up. That is why Aunt Buck and Uncle Levi lived in Chattanooga.

Uncle Levi and Aunt Buck many years later holding my son Steve.

FROM TENNESSEE TO OKLAHOMA

After some time, my mother and I rode the bus to Beggs, Oklahoma to live with another of Mother's sisters, Aunt Mary Dee, who had four girls living in a small house. What are two more anyway? My mother got a job at Hughes Aircraft in Tulsa working nights while I slept. My mother worked using a rivet gun to attach wings, etc. to planes. During World War II most men went to war. Women came forward to do what had always been men's work in factories. These jobs were making things needed in the war. They were helping in the war effort. The ladies in these jobs were called "Rosie the Riveter". Before the war, there were not many jobs for women outside of the home.

A little while later, we moved back in with my mother's parents. She paid someone who also worked at Hughes in Tulsa for rides to work. Again, she worked nights while my grandmother watched me. Mother's sisters, Delia, and her daughter, Jenney, were also living at Grandma and Grandpa's farm. My cousin Jenney was my first playmate. She has always been so special to me. I have fond memories of that time with so many living in that little farmhouse. Now we think we need such big houses with lots of bathrooms. We all lived in four rooms with no bathrooms.

I was only two years old when we lived with my grandparents in Nuyaka, but I remember small pieces of events of that time. I remember being in a small, one-room church. As the minister finished his sermon, a beautiful young bride came down the aisle in a white wedding dress. That was the first wedding I attended.

One night, Mother and I were in a car with two other people. This car kept dying. The man driving would get out and wind it up in front. Eventually, we got back to my grandparents' house. I just remember the man kept getting out and winding the car.

When we came back to Oklahoma, Aunt Buck and Uncle Levi moved from Chattanooga to a little house across the road from my grandparents. They had two boys several years older than me. I remember the two boys carrying me all over the farm. There were steps to go over the fence. You would walk up three steps and down three steps to get over the fence. One of them set me over the fence and then walked up and down these steps to get to the other side. The problem was the place they set me was in the middle of a big red ant bed. I remember that very well. I was bitten all over. My poor cousin cried because he felt so bad for me. He loved me. I always had so many people who loved me.

Aunt Buck and Uncle Levi moved back to Chattanooga after the war and lived there until their death. We did visit them several times over the years. Barry and I later took the three boys to visit them in Chattanooga.

One of the saddest things to me is that I am an only child. I am so thankful to God that my mother was not an only child. What would have happened to Mother and me during the war if she had been an only child? My mother always paid the families to live with them. That helped them with money also.

THE WAR WAS OVER

On Christmas Day 1945, my dad came home to us at my grandparents' house. He had hitched a ride with someone and everyone ran to the car. I remember crawling upon the couch and on my knees, I looked out the window. Aunt Delia came running back to tell me to come out and see my dad. I told her that was not my dad. I had carried a picture of my dad in his sailor uniform for over a year. That man did not have on a sailor uniform so he could not be my dad. I finally did have to accept the fact that he was my dad because everyone I knew kept telling me that he was my dad.

CHAPTER 2

We Became Farmers

My mother had rented a very little house down the road from my grandparents. She had bought a couch and chair, a table and china cabinet, their bed and a baby bed for me. We lived there until we found a farm to rent.

The farm we found was outside of Morris, close to my dad's two brothers. With all the men coming home from the war, it was hard to find farms to rent. This house had no electricity, no well and the stool of the outhouse had no walls. My dad built walls and a roof for more privacy. My mother had saved money from her working while Dad was away to buy cows and chickens. We were a working farm.

We had an ice box which kept milk and meat. We killed and dressed chickens and took them into Morris where we had rented a locker at the ice house. Each week we would go to the ice house in Morris to get ice and meat to bring home for meals for that week. The ice and meat would go into the ice box. Most days we had pinto beans and cornbread.

I remember a very bad winter week that had deep snow and ice. We could not get to our locker in town. I looked out the back door and saw a bucket with snow and birds in it. My dad had shot the birds for us to eat that week. We dealt with life as best we could! I am so thankful for the lessons that I learned at such a young age.

Each Saturday we went to the big town of Okmulgee. At the fire station we filled milk cans with water to use the next week. We sold Mother's chicken eggs. I fondly remember that every Saturday we went to the restaurant to eat a hamburger and ice cream cone. What a treat Saturday was!

I usually had a nickel or dime to take to Kress Five & Dime store. I always took a long time to choose what I wanted to buy. One Saturday there was a long, long line outside of Kress. We did not know why. We could not get into the store except by getting into the line. We slowly moved down the sidewalk and finally into the store.

THE MARCH OF DIMES

As we moved into the store we went past a lady in an iron lung. The top of the iron lung was glass so she could see her surroundings and the machine was pressurized so she could breathe. She had polio.

Polio was a really bad disease which sometimes left people unable to walk and not able to breathe. The purpose of the parade by the iron lung was to educate people about this terrible illness. There was no TV to learn about such things. Also as you walked by the iron lung, you were to put a dime in a container. The money was to help fight the disease and to pay for research for a cure.

This organization became known as the March of Dimes. The name came from the march by the iron lung and the dimes paid by the people who marched by. The March of Dimes still exists to collect money to fight other illnesses. Children were the most likely to get polio. President Roosevelt did have polio as an adult and had leg braces for the rest of his life.

When Barry and I first married and lived in Houston, we stood in a long line to go into a tent. We received the Salk vaccination for polio. Dr. Salk and his vaccine put an end to polio. Still today, children receive the Salk vaccine as babies to prevent this disease. Our shot was free. The sign in the tent said, "Paid for by the March of Dimes."

SEWING TOOK TWO PEOPLE

My mother and I made us matching dresses. Mother had a sewing machine that was a portable (not a treadle sewing machine). I would sit on the table and turn the knob on the wheel while Mother guided the fabric. It took a long time to make those two dresses. My arm would get tired. I was only three years old. I loved doing it. Oh, how I loved those matching dresses!

Flour was bought in printed cotton fabric sacks. You would pick out a print fabric you liked and hopefully that same print fabric could be bought several times. Then you would make a dress.

LINE UP FOR YOUR PUNISHMENT

There was a family with many kids who lived down the road from me. They lived down yonder past the cotton field. I love the word "yonder." One time I went down to play. There was a girl one year older than me and one who was one year younger than me. They were very poor but we had so much fun playing together that I thought that they were rich.

On one visit, one or maybe several of the kids had put their mother over

Mother and me in matching dresses made by my hand turning the wheel.

the edge. She said that they all, except the baby, had to line up in front of her. Each one got two smacks on the bottom as they got to her lap. The two older boys held me in the line for my turn. They were laughing so hard. I finally got on all fours on the floor and climbed between the legs of several before I managed to get out of their reach and headed out the door. I ran all the way home with my heart beating so fast! I had just arrived when the lineup was ordered. I knew that I had done nothing for which I should be punished. I had just gotten there. I was so scared then, but now the memory makes me smile.

NO TV, JUST WONDERFUL PEOPLE

Mrs. Ashley lived down the road a ways from our house. She was a good friend to me and brought so much light into my life. She was my older friend who always had time to spend with me. She was a widow and her son was away in the Army at that time.

Mrs. Ashley had every animal you could imagine. She even had a pet skunk that had been deodorized. I loved to go down and help her feed all her animals. She had ducks and cows and all in between. She farmed the farm herself, and I am sure she had plenty to do without me showing up to visit and take her time. I guess my parents thought I was so great that everyone was sure to be happy to see me.

Mrs. Ashley's front yard was a big flower garden. I loved everything about being with my older friend. We sometimes worked in the flower garden. Maybe my love of my flower gardens started in Mrs. Ashley's front yard.

One visit was a bit stressful. Mrs. Ashley was putting a new roof on a small barn. I went up on the roof with her. I handed the shingles to her. I jumped off the roof to the ground with my foot landing on an old shingle with a nail sticking up. It went deep into my foot.

Mrs. Ashley was afraid my parents would be upset. They told her not to worry about it because I was always doing something like that. A little alcohol on it and away I went. We didn't go to doctors. I think I just developed a good immune system. I remember I was not going to cry because I did not want Mrs. Ashley to feel bad.

Mrs. Ashley had a strong faith. She worked hard but was always happy for me to be with her. She farmed by herself, but also made time to work on the flower gardens.

Mrs. Ashley's well was under her kitchen sink. There was a red pump that emptied into her kitchen sink. That was the nearest thing to a modern convenience she had in her life.

Barry and I took Curtis and Keith back to see Mrs. Ashley many years later. She had a pet squirrel in a big cage. She gave the two boys a wrapped piece of candy. They gave it to the squirrel. The squirrel unwrapped and ate that candy in no time at all. She was older but still the same sweet lady. I thank God I had Mrs. Ashley in my life. She, along with many others, made my roots grow deep.

GOOD AND BAD TIMES ON THE FARM

One morning we woke up to find all our cows dead in a pool of saltwater. Men were drilling a well there. I don't remember if it was an oil well or a water well, but it got saltwater, which our cows had drunk, killing them all. What a hard blow.

After a year or so, my dad's brother bought a bigger house with running water down the road from where he had been living. We moved into the house where he and family had lived. We thought we had died and gone to heaven. This house had three bedrooms, electricity and an indoor bathroom. The problem was that there was no running water. The bathroom was nice just to have. We continued to get water at the fire station every Saturday. We could not get a refrigerator even though we had electricity, so we had to continue to use the ice box for meat. No refrigerators were made during the war because factories were all making things for the war. We put our names on a waiting list to get a refrigerator now that we had electricity.

This farm had been a dairy farm and had huge dairy barns and lots of milk cans. I played in those barns for hours at a time. I would arrange the milk cans in a way that designed walls and doors. This was my playhouse. My dolls were my playmates. I talked a lot to them. It takes a lot of imagination for an only child living on a farm.

I would swing on the swing my father put on a limb of a big tree. I would watch above as the Oklahoma wind moved clouds in the sky. I would find rooms in the clouds to decorate in my mind. I have always loved to decorate even when I did not have a house in which to put my decorating ideas.

I woke up one morning and it was a beautiful morning. I was so happy and I did not know why. I have always been happy unless something really bad is weighing on my mind. That is a gift from God, and I am thankful for that gift. I went out on the back step and sat down. I talked to God about this wonderful day. Then I looked out across the back yard which was covered with chicken poop. No one would walk across that yard without messing up their shoes. My mother would cut off the top third of my shoes when the weather was warm enough. My toes could grow out over the sole making my shoes last longer. I was in shoes ready for the warm weather. These shoes would not protect my toes from chicken poop in that yard. I kept smelling something that really smelled good, not like chicken poop. I looked to the other side of the back yard and there growing on a fence was honeysuckle in bloom. I used to ride on that vine on the fence pretending it was my horse. But now it had thousands of blooms. There was a brisk wind blowing that honeysuckle smell over that chicken poop. I could not smell the chicken poop but just honeysuckle.

I started designing flower beds in my mind. I even planned what flowers I would plant in these beds along the back of the house. I remember thanking God for that wind blowing the honeysuckle smell to me. Then I remember telling God I must be crazy sitting here in all this chicken poop and being so happy. Then I got up and went in the house and out the front door so I could walk out to play without getting chicken poop on my toes.

I always had worn White Shoulders perfume. It smelled like honeysuckle blossoms. After all these years, White Shoulders perfume was discontinued a few years ago. I guess most of the old women like me who remembered fondly the scent of honeysuckle blossoms have died.

BEES IN THE WALLS

We got bees living in the exterior walls of our house. These bees made honey inside the walls. I picked up a spoon to eat my oatmeal. A bee was on the bottom of the spoon. That was my first bee sting.

My parents took me to stay with my grandmother. I think there were bees all inside the house before it was over.

My dad's brother kept bees. He brought a smoker and his other equipment and marched them to his beehives.

GAMES FARM GIRLS PLAY

My cousin Patti (Patsy then) lived just down the road. It was the only house to be seen from our house. Patti had two big sisters, but Patti and I were only a few months apart in age. We played together a lot.

We made wonderful pretend meals. We made green beans from the beans on Catalpa trees in the yard. I have a Catalpa tree in my back yard now so I can show my grandchildren the pretend green beans.

Patti and I made great mud pies. We made them with mud and water and then put them in the sun to harden. One day we found some eggs in the loft of a big barn where we were playing. We tried to take them to her mother (My Aunt Ola). Aunt Ola was mopping the floors. The floors were all wet so she would not let us in. I don't remember which one of us came up with the idea to make mud pies with eggs in them. We both thought this was a great idea, so we used all of the eggs in our mud pies. They made wonderful mud pies. Aunt Ola did not think this was a good idea at all.

She sold her eggs every Saturday in Okmulgee as my mother did. Aunt Ola died a few years ago at 98 years old. We made a trip to Oklahoma to see her a few months before she died. She always laughed and brought up the egg filled mud pies when we were together. I cook a lot of Aunt Ola's recipes now. They are all so good, but of course, none have mud in the recipes. I do always think about our egg mud pies and smile when I use one of her recipes. Such wonderful memories!

SUMMER BROUGHT VACATION BIBLE SCHOOL

The church in Morris was one of my favorite places to be. My favorite was Vacation Bible School. It was the highlight of my life. We played games with everyone in a big circle: Farmer in the Dell, Drop the Handkerchief, etc. I had never heard of such games. My love of Vacation Bible School lasted into old age. I taught Vacation Bible School for over 33 years.

One Sunday my friend was going home with a different friend after church. I had planned on her coming home with me. I was crying. The pastor of the church was walking behind my mother and me. He told my mother that his two girls would really like for me to come to their house to play for the afternoon. I was so happy and excited, and I still remember that feeling I had that day. My pastor was my friend! One should never minimize the difference kind words can make when said to children. The opposite difference can be made by unkind words said to a child.

In Sunday school, teachers would use flannel boards with Bible pictures backed in flannel. The pictures would stick to the board as the teacher moved them around to illustrate the Bible story she was telling. It was very low tech, but it impressed this little farm girl. My roots did grow deeper still.

Barry and I visited our grandson, Tyler, some time ago in Oklahoma where he was working at the time. We took him on a small tour of my hometown and two-room school and my church in Morris. I knew the house and the school were gone but did not know that the old church building was gone. It hurt my heart to see that empty lot. There are other new buildings built for the church.

The old church had many steps going up to the sanctuary. The lower floor was half underground. That was where Sunday school met. This church was the biggest and oldest building in Morris. I saw Mrs. Ashley's son at an Evening Star reunion. He said it was going to cost $30,000 to put a new roof on and it cost $30,000 to tear down the old building. The decision was to tear it down. It had no air conditioning except the fans on a stick sitting in the pews.

I can still hear the old, old hymns being sung in that building. It was always the highlight of my week. As I write this today, tears are going down my cheeks. I thank God for the time I had in those pews fanning with the fans on a stick. The fans had such pretty pictures on them.

CHAPTER 3

Evening Star

The summer when I was five years old Mr. Ford came to visit us. Mr. Ford was the principal and one of three teachers at Evening Star School. The school needed 50 pupils to stay open. They had 49. He wanted to know if I would like to start to school early. I would not be six years old until January of the first grade. Since my parents thought I was so, so smart, that would be a wonderful idea. As an only child, they had no other child to compare me to. Of course, I was excited. Evening Star was one mile down the road. I had three cousins in the school and my dad had spent the first grade there.

Evening Star was one large room with a folding wall in the center making two rooms with a stage in front. There was a coat room in the front. Each grade had a row of desks. My first-grade class had six kids in our row. The "little room" was four rows for first through fourth grade. The "big room" had four rows of larger desks for the fifth through eighth grade. After eighth everyone went to high school in the town of Morris.

There were two outhouses. One for boys and one for girls. The girl's outhouse had two stools. I don't know how many were in the boy's. At the back of the school there was one bucket of water brought by a teacher each day. The bucket had one dipper in it. We all washed our hands in the same little pan with a little water in it. We all used the same dipper to drink water. None of us ever got sick. I was an adult with children when I got measles and chicken pox. My kids and I had them together.

I loved this school. My teacher, Mrs. Williams, was so kind and loving. I only had one bad episode with kids in this school. I will tell you about that later. The kids were all farm kids who showed respect for the teacher and other students. The parents all knew the teachers well and would have always taken the teacher's side if there had been a problem.

There was no lunchroom when I started to school there. We all brought our lunches. Sometime that year some of the fathers went someplace to take down a building which was free. They took down the wood building and loaded it on big farm trucks. They brought it back and put it back together behind the brick schoolhouse for a lunchroom. One of the fathers died during this undertaking when one of the walls fell on him. He had three children. One girl was one year younger than me. That girl was my cousin, Patti's best friend all through high school. So, so sad!

My dad in first grade at Evening Star. He is the fifth one from the left on the first row.

Evening Star second grade picture. I am in the middle row on the right end.

LUNCH AT EVENING STAR

The mother of one of my classmates walked from her house to the school each morning and cooked for all 53 of us. Usually she cooked a big, big pot of soup and cornbread or a big pot of pinto beans and cornbread. I still have in my house one of the bowls and a glass we used. We also got a glass of milk or water. On Friday she would cook fried chicken.

The girls who wanted to do it would sweep the floor after lunch for a week. They would receive a small gift. I finally received this honor when I was in the third grade. I received a bottle of "Evening in Paris" cologne. That was one of the first colognes to be made. I was so, so happy.

NO RHYTHM

The whole school put on a Christmas program for the parents. We had a rhythm band where each grade played a different instrument. The first grade did sticks. I was so proud at first. But try as I might, I could never hit the sticks at the same time as my classmates. Mrs. Williams tried her best to help me. Finally, she asked me to just pretend to hit my sticks. This was my first time of many times to realize that I had no musical talent whatsoever.

My lack of musical talent is one of the biggest disappointments of my life. When we clap at church with a song, I remember to pretend to clap. I can't carry a tune and never know by listening if other people are in tune with the group. I sing very softly in church so no one can hear me. But in the car with the radio playing off of Barry's phone a long list of the old hymns, I sing as loud as I want to sing. I know all the words. I tell my grandchildren that believe it or not, to God and me, that my singing is a joyful noise. I am sure they are glad to get wherever we are going so that they can get out of the car.

PUBLIC CHRISTIAN SCHOOL

Before there were schools called private Christian schools, Evening Star was a public Christian School. The play put on at Christmas was "The Christmas Guest." Sometime everyone should listen to the "Christmas Guest" recorded by Johnny Cash. The old man wants Jesus to be his guest for Christmas dinner. He asked Jesus at the end of the day why He had not come. Jesus tells him that He kept His word. He came once as the beggar with bruised, cold feet and He came as a woman you gave something to eat. Jesus came as the child on the homeless street. Three times he knocked and three times He came in. And each time I found the warmth of a friend. Of all the gifts, love is the best, and I was honored to be your Christmas guest.

A few years after my dad's return from war, we were fighting another war with Korea. I remember hearing about it on the radio. Mother had met a lady and her young child who lived down the road a couple miles. Her husband was away at war. He was at a prisoner of war camp in North Korea. The lady and her child lived in a trailer behind her husband's parents' house. I remember her going to the Evening Star Christmas program with us on Christmas Eve. I remember bringing her home and seeing her alone carrying her child down the drive and into her trailer. I remember thinking what a sad thing. But she had enjoyed the school program.

The husband did make it home after the war. He had survived by eating tree bark and grass. Most of the men died. They were not fed in the prisoner of war camp. Many years later I saw him and his wife at a family funeral. He was a smiling happy man. In my mind I recall his wife and child walking alone to the trailer that Christmas Eve. What a wonderful play the kids preformed for Christmas. Please read the whole play sometime. You will be blessed. Your roots will grow deeper too.

EASTER AT EVENING STAR

On the last day of school before Easter, Mrs. Williams called the first-grade class to the front to sit in chairs in a circle. Mrs. Williams sat in the middle on a chair with the Bible open in her lap and three crosses.

She read the Easter story from the Bible and showed us the crosses. She told us of the two men on each side of Jesus. She told us of the grave which could not hold Jesus. She told us we would have to make a decision someday of whether we wanted to take Jesus as our Lord and Savior. She told us we would need to study the Bible to know the path Jesus would want us to take in our lives.

I have never had one moment of doubt of all she told us since that day. My roots grew deeper!

Lots of people do have doubts and have to work things out in their minds and hearts. I am so thankful that I have not had to work out doubts. I have had lots of hard times that I have not understood, but I always knew that Jesus was there with me during those hard times. The more I have learned (DNA, etc), the more God is the only answer.

PIE SUPPERS

Once a year Evening Star had a pie supper to raise money. All the women made a pie for themselves to take and one for each schoolgirl to take. These would be auctioned off to the men and boys.

The men and boys did not know who made the pie until they bought it in the auction. The boys and men would eat some of the pie with the maker of the pie. The boys and men got to take home the remaining pie. A boy in the eighth grade bought my pie. He was so nice and visited with me while we ate pie. What a wonderful memory.

ONE SAD MEMORY

When I started each morning to school, I would join other kids as they got to my corner to walk the mile to school. There were two large families with kids of all ages in this group.

My mother had bought me three pair of silky panties when I started to school. She would wash them out and hang them over the claw footed tub at night to dry. All the girls in these large farm families wore bloomers made by their mothers from flour sacks. One day a couple of the larger boys in the group pushed me down in the ditch and pulled up my dress to show everyone my fancy panties. First of all, I was scared. As an only child, I had never hit or pushed anyone, nor had anyone ever done this to me.

I remember crying, but most of all, I remember being so embarrassed for everyone to know how rich I was. I didn't want the girls to feel badly about their flour sack bloomers. I did not want them to know that I was rich.

The next day I did not want to go to school. My mother met the kids the next morning and told them they should be ashamed for picking on a five-year-old. That night their mother and dad came to our house to talk to my mother and dad. I did go back to school and no one ever showed anyone else my panties again. But I still felt bad about being rich.

CLASSMATES

One night I spent the night with my good friend Kay. She had lots of brothers and sisters. We played a game in an upstairs bedroom where there were lots of beds against the walls. In between the beds against the walls were large toe sacks full of unshelled peanuts. We all played a tag game jumping from one sack and across the beds to the next sack. One was chasing all the others. If you fell off the sacks or the bed to the floor, you were out of the game. If the one chasing the others touched you that meant you were out of the game. To me, this was as much fun as I could ever remember having.

I thought they were so lucky having so many brothers and sisters and toe sacks of peanuts in their bedroom. I recalled this memory to Kay and her sister at an Evening Star reunion a few years ago. Her sister said as she laughed that they just called these toe sacks furniture. At breakfast the next morning, we had homemade biscuits and chocolate gravy. I had never had chocolate gravy and thought that I must be in heaven. This family who had very little seemed to have everything to me. They had all they needed with their loving family and chocolate gravy.

All the kids from Evening Star who I know of grew up to be good, self-reliant adults. So many grew up in the little farming community with few material things. Their parents were hard working, loving people who wanted their kids to grow up to be a help to society and not a drag on society. From the ones I know about, the parents' dreams came true.

Kay went to college when her kids went to school and taught school in Morris until she retired. At that time, the superintendent of Morris School District was one of my older classmates at Evening Star. One of my cousins at Evening Star taught in Morris for years. The State Representative of that district was one grade below me at Evening Star.

One of the girls from Evening Star became a great seamstress and I heard she has a good business designing and sewing girls' dance costumes.

I spent the night with another girlfriend named Wanda. It was a Saturday night. We were talking and I heard a loud voice from the next room singing hymns. I looked around the corner to see her father singing with a hymn book in one hand and the other hand going up and down leading music. Wanda told me that he led the singing at her church and practiced every Saturday night.

My father would never attend church with my mother and me. His brothers and all their families went every Sunday. I just thought how lucky Wanda was that her father went to church with her and led the music. I would have been so proud. I vowed that I would not marry a man who would not go to church with me. And I did not do that. I am so thankful on Sunday mornings to sit in a long row of my family. I feel so blessed.

CHAPTER 4

Cotton and Peanuts

I went to the fields with my mother and father to gather the crops. After a long sweaty day of shaking peanuts we came home with our faces covered with dirt except our eyes. The wind blows a lot in Oklahoma. The wind blew the dirt all over us and it stuck to our sweaty bodies. We had to wash outside before we could come into the screened back porch to take a bath in the big #2 tub.

When the cotton was ready to be picked, my dad went to the area in Okmulgee to pick up people to help. These were all black people ready to make some money. They would fill their big bags full and go to my dad who was standing by the big truck. The scales were on the big truck. The pickers were paid by the pound. Sometimes he would find a rock or two in the bag to make it weigh more. This didn't happen all the time.

My mother made my bag with a toe sack with one of her hose tied on each side. The hose would go around my neck with the toe sack hanging under my arm. Once I got thirsty and was running to the truck for a drink of water. As I jumped over each row, I sometimes would pick a cotton ball and put it in my sack. As I was making my way to the water, I heard a loud scream coming from a large woman coming down the row I had just jumped over. She said, "You little white-headed girl better get off my row. Don't you pick cotton off my row!" Her eyes were very large white with black pupils. As I looked at her, those eyes seemed to be jumping from her head right toward me. I think I stayed in the truck the rest of the day. I was scared. I don't think I was much help with the cotton picking.

THE BIG HUDSON CAR

One day as I came out of the doors of Evening Star to go home, there was a crowd of everyone in the school. They were all crowded around a big car.

All the kids in this school were from families with large farm trucks. No one had a car. It turned out to be my Aunt Ola in a big Hudson they had just bought. An identical car was used in the movie "Driving Miss Daisy" many years later. Uncle Carl, my dad's brother, was a hard worker and had run a dairy during World War II. He owned his own farmland and was proud to be able to buy his wife such a car!

MY MOTHER GOES BACK TO SCHOOL

In Okmulgee during World War II, a prisoner of war hospital was built. After the war, it became a state vocational school. My mother started going to the school to learn typing, shorthand and other secretarial skills. She was starting to read the writing on the wall that farming might not be the answer she had hoped.

My mother was very self-driven in whatever she did. At night she would write in shorthand with her finger in the air everything my dad and I would say. She would stay up late studying her bookkeeping. My dad and I would go to bed leaving her up to study. Dad would write on my little blackboard, "Goodnight Irene." Irene was her name, and that song was the number one song on the radio at that time.

As my mother was growing up, she sometimes lived too far from a school for her to be able to attend a school. The family moved to a farm to Nuyaka which was a short distance from a school. Her dad told her that she could not go to school any longer. Her dad had never gone to school in his life and thought it was a way to get out of doing work. She would hide in a ditch and jump up when she saw the school bus. He would chase the bus down the road, but she went to school. He gave up and she did graduate from high school.

MY DAD WAS NOT A SELF-DRIVEN MAN

My dad had a lot of good traits, and I loved him. My dad was the last born in his family. He was cute and had very curly hair and was jovial. He made everyone around him have fun unless someone around him was trying to make him do something he did not want to do, like maybe work. He would give anyone who needed it his last few dollars even though it would mean that he could not pay the rent the next day.

He would tell the doctors that he had a heart attack when he was 12 years old. Every doctor I took him to would say his heart showed that he had never had a heart attack. I would have to take the doctor aside to explain that there was no point in trying to convince my dad of that.

He would tell you that the doctor gave him a shot on the sidewalk outside the office. That shot saved his life. This all did happen, but it was no heart attack, and the shot did not save his life. He was ordered to spend two years in bed after this event. My Aunt Lorah, Dad's sister, said their mother would make her get out of bed to make him a pie at midnight if he wanted a pie. No one could dare upset him because he might have another heart attack. So my dad got what he wanted when he wanted it. Otherwise, he might have a heart attack!

At 14 years old, Everett decided he no longer could stand to attend school. One of his brothers would tell about hitching up the wagon and taking Everett to school. When his brother got back to the house, my dad would be on the front porch laughing. He had cut through the fields to make it home before his brother with the wagon.

At this same time my dad had been visiting a full-blooded Indian man down the road. This Indian was old and had no family. My dad sometimes helped him and would visit. My dad kept the Indian man laughing a lot. This man became very fond of my dad. He told my dad that he wanted to adopt him and would leave his great farm to him. My dad was ready to move in with him and be his son if his family continued insisting that he go to school. So, my dad quit school at age 14.

LIFE IS FOR THE PLAYING

My dad would play marbles with me on the linoleum floors of the farmhouse. He would draw a circle with chalk on the floor and we would shoot marbles. One day my mother was upset over some mess my dad and I had made. She told me that next time this happened she was going to spank me. My dad told me to tell her, "Always next time, never this time." I was dumb enough to tell her that! I knew after one look on her face, I was in lots of trouble.

Dad was laughing so hard. I was trying to explain that dad had told me to say that. I had a broom in my hands, and I swung it at him. I thought over his head. He stood up just as I swung the broom.

It hit him on the top of his head really hard. A big bump came up almost instantly. I didn't know who to run from! They both started laughing, for I looked petrified. I know that Mother thought she had two children living in the house with her. Dad and I had lots of fun together during those years.

FAMILY: GOD'S GREATEST GIFT

Three out of four of my mother's brothers were bad alcoholics. These brothers were always welcome to holidays at my grandmother's house if they were not drinking. They usually did not join us. My mother and her sisters loved those brothers no matter what they did.

The brothers lost their families while their kids were young. They were often violent when they drank. I remember waking up in the middle of the night and getting dressed and going to Okmulgee to bail out one of these drunk uncles. I remember going to state prison to visit one of these uncles. I remember the big door closing and locking as we went into the visitation room. I remember driving to California when I was 16 years old. We had our first new car. It was the first time we had a car good enough to make that long of a trip. The car was a pretty flamingo pink and white Ford. I got to pick out the color! Of course, there was no car air conditioning. The hot desert was so hot. Once we stopped at a bus station to go into the bathrooms and splash cold water over our hair and bodies.

The main purposes of this trip was to visit one of the uncles who was in a Tuberculosis (TB) sanitarium. The patients could not leave because they might give other people TB. As I walked into the long barracks – with men in beds down both walls – I wondered what was keeping us from catching TB. I still don't know the answer to that question.

One of the brothers fell over my grandmother's casket at her funeral. He was allowed to come to his mother's funeral even if he was drinking. His sisters still loved him. Hating him would not have helped him stop drinking.

Going through my mother's papers after she died, I found many letters to her from her brothers thanking her for the five or ten dollars she had sent them while they were in VA hospitals, jail or wherever. She did not have a lot of money.

My mother and her sisters did not agree at all with the lives these brothers lived. They still loved their brothers and the brothers always knew this. The brothers all died in their early 50s from the toll alcohol took on their bodies.

One brother in California was about to be buried in a pauper's grave because no one had claimed his body. My mother tracked him down. The sisters went together and flew his body home and buried him by their parents. He had not seen his parents since he was in his 20s, over 30 years earlier.

I learned a lot about loving family growing up watching these sisters' love for their brothers. I may not like every trait of a family nor will I like everything said to me by any family member, but they are my family. I will love them and do all I can for them. They do not have to show any appreciation or love for me. I will love them. Probably loving them will help me more than them.

I am sure I have traits that family members do not like, much less love. I pray that they will spread a little grace and forgiveness over the problem and love me anyway. I have seen people think that they need to tell every family member every small thing they do not like about that family member. More than likely, that family member can come up with a longer list of things they do not like about them. I have seen so many relationships never recover from these encounters. Family gatherings can become smaller and smaller because of lack of grace, mercy and forgiveness.

> Love suffers long *and* is kind; love does not envy; love does not parade itself, is not puffed up; does not behave rudely, does not seek its own, is not provoked, thinks no evil; does not rejoice in iniquity, but rejoices in the truth; bears all things, believes all things, hopes all things, endures all things. Love never fails. (1 Corinthians 13:4-8a NKJV)

CHAPTER 5

An Abrupt End

The government would pay for further education for the GIs after the war. My dad went to farming school two nights a week. He got a check once a month from the government. When the time was up, the checks quit coming. You can live off of what you produce on a farm, but you need some cash to buy gas, pay electric, buy shoes, pay rent, pay for the farm, etc.

We had one cow that was producing milk which was sold. My dad got tired of getting up so early to milk the cow, so he let her go dry. No more money from the sale of milk.

My dad's brother told my mother that we were all going to starve if she did not get his brother off the farm. She agreed and my idyllic life of the little farm girl living with cousins down the road both ways and my wonderful two-room school came to an abrupt end.

We gave away our little bit of furniture, sold our tractor and put what clothes we had along with a few belongings in the back of our farm truck. We moved to Fort Worth where my dad's sister, Aunt Larah, her husband, and her daughter lived in a duplex of three rooms with a bathroom.

We slept on the floor until my mother and father could find some work. My mother said she knew that Aunt Larah would not let us starve. Dad's father died when he was 16. His mother died when he was 18. Aunt Larah had always taken care of her little brother, until my mother took over that job. After all, if she had not, he might have had a heart attack!

THE MIRACLE OF MY DEEP ROOTS

I have said so many times that my roots grew deep in those first eight years. I had family living in two different houses on the same road I lived on. For holidays we went to my mother's parents and were with so many cousins. One of my greatest memories of my childhood was holidays with all the family.

We had to take turns eating. Kids ate first and then washed and dried dishes together for the next group to use. We had to heat the water on the stove to wash the dishes. Everybody brought food. It was so crowded that men would take turns putting on coats and going to the front porch. My grandparents had more than 27 grandchildren. There were five girl cousins within two years of my age. We had so much fun. Everyone enjoyed it so much. No one thought it was a problem to be crowded and so many children.

I always felt so close to my cousins and my aunts and uncles. Barry and I have taken many trips to visit my aunts and uncles as they aged, and they were always so glad to see us. Without all those crowded family gatherings they would not have even known me, much less loved me. One of God's greatest gifts is family. Enjoy them.

I was nurtured by family, my church, my little school, my older friend Mrs. Ashley and everyone I knew. I see God's fingerprints through it all. God knew I would need this strong foundation when we left the farm, entering a new life with more problems than I ever dreamed.

Cousins that lived on my road: Helen, Prue, Donna, and Patty – boy not related.

Aunt Lorah was my dad's sister and somewhat like a grandmother on Dad's side. Aunt Lorah and Uncle JT had a television. I had never seen one. I loved watching Howdy Doody Time. We stayed with Aunt Lorah for a brief period when we first moved to Fort Worth.

ALWAYS THANKFUL FOR NEW FRIENDS

There was a girl my age living across the street. Her name was Kaylyn. This is the first miracle of many a friend waiting for me each time I moved to a new location. We were in the same class for two years. We became very good friends. Friends can make such a difference in our lives in a new location. Kaylyn was the only child who lived on Aunt Lorah's street that was my age.

It was Christmas when we moved to Texas. Aunt Lorah took me to toy land in Leonard's Department Store in Fort Worth. We went down moving stairs. I had never seen anything like toy land or moving stairs. I was amazed!

My dad got a job with a friend of Uncle JT's. They put hot tar on roofs and put small white stones on the hot tar. He came home with new bad burns on his arms each night where the hot tar got on him.

Aunt Lorah lived in the Riverside area of Fort Worth, and it was not a rich side of Fort Worth. But even I did notice very quickly that I was no longer rich.

My mother got a job at a 5 & 10 cent store. We moved into two small rooms at the back of a house. We had three cardboard boxes with the tops cut on three sides. They were about 14 inches tall. The top flipped up for us to get our underwear out. We each had our names on the front of the three boxes. There was a small closet to put our clothes in. There was a bed for my mother and father. At the end of the bed, I would put up an army cot each night. It touched the wall on one side and bed on the other. We used a bathroom that we shared with the people who lived in the front of the house.

When my dad needed to go to the bathroom during the night, I would have to get up and hold my cot on the end for him to get by to the door opening into the hall where the bathroom was. There was a kitchen with a sink, a stove, a small refrigerator and a tiny table with two chairs. The store where my mother worked was close enough for her to walk to work. After school I would walk with Kaylyn to Aunt Lorah's house.

SCHOOL MEMORIES

At Evening Star School, we played at recess on the merry-go-round. Here at Riverside Elementary School, the girls played jump rope. A girl on each end held the rope and swung it around. The other girl was to run in and jump the rope.

I was a miserable failure at this. All the other girls could all do this with no trouble. They thought it was funny that I could not do this. I did not think it was funny.

Mother and Dad got a rope and spent hours in the back yard with my trying to run in without falling on my face. I am sure they were tired after working on their feet all day. It took doing this every night for many nights, but I did get to where I could do it. We were all much happier.

In February, when the rodeo was going on in Fort Worth, school had Western Day. I knew it was Western Day at school. I did not know what that meant.

Uncle JT came to pick me up and took me to a store and got me a cowboy hat and handkerchief for my neck. He then took me to school a little late. I guess he was off work that day or took off. I tell you this to tell all of you how important families are. They can even sometimes smooth out the rough spots in the life of a little girl trying to adjust from farm girl to city girl.

COLD WAR WITH RUSSIA

Russia was the first country after the United States to develop the Atomic Bomb. The Cold War was in full swing while I was at Riverside Elementary. A certain bell would sound. We knew to get under our desks and cover our heads with our hands. This was practice in case Fort Worth was ever bombed. This was called duck and cover.

There was another bell signal that sent us outside the school. Each child was given a place next to the circle on our given street. We were to line up there to get in a car to be taken to a designated place out of the city. Mothers who were at home and had a car were assigned a spot to pick up the children for the trip out of town.

Each child knew where to go and the name of the mother who would take them out of town. The mothers who did not pick-up children were told where their child would be taken. We would all practice this when the proper bell rang. We went to our spot and got in the proper car. We did not leave in the car for a practice. Think about this when you think you live under too much stress.

THE MIRACLE OF NEIGHBORS

After several months, Mother got a job at Convair where they made B36 airplanes. She worked on big rivet machines on the assembly line.

We were able to rent a white house on a short street with other little, tiny houses. It is kind of unforgettable the wonderful people who seemed to be placed there to take care of our needs. God is so good.

Mother paid a man at the end of the street for a ride to Convair where he also worked. His wife kept me with her son and daughter that summer between my third and fourth grade. We had so much fun together. I got a nickel each day for the ice cream man who came by every day.

We went to Bible School for two weeks that summer. I loved that. One day I was told to wear nice clothes the next day because we were to go downtown. The lady dressed up with a hat, high heel shoes and white gloves. This is how women dressed to go downtown in the 1950s. We walked to the end of the street to the big street and caught the bus for downtown. That was a big deal and good memory.

When school started, Mother paid a woman at the corner of our street and the big street to keep me until my ride to school came by. Another mother picked me up for the ride to school. This lady had a daughter in my class. Mother gave me the money to pay her each Friday. The lady with whom I stayed waiting for my ride to school loved to make big bows to put in my hair each morning. They were pretty bows, but no girls wore big bows in their hair. She had different bows to match my outfit each day. I would take them off in the car before I got to school, but I appreciated her love.

There was a girl about 15 years old across the street from my house who taught me to crochet. I made a big doily with her help. Doilies were used a lot then. I was so proud of my big doily. That was a big deal.

She also taught me to make clothes for my doll. We sewed by hand with needle and thread. She was such a nice girl and enjoyed teaching me and I enjoyed learning from her.

There were lots of kids on our street. I went trick-or-treating with them on Halloween. I had never heard of trick-or-treating. Needless to say, I loved it.

On that little street there were so many people there to meet all our needs. To me it was one of God's miracles to have so many people in a few houses around our house who supplied all our needs. I see God's fingerprints in at all. This little house was only maybe 500 square feet and no garage. We had a nice back yard with some very large trees. We had an inside bathroom for just us and with running water.

Unfortunately, we were not able to stay there very long. My mother got pregnant but was not able to carry the baby to term. She ended up in the hospital and missed a lot of work. We could not afford our little white house anymore.

HALF OF A HOUSE

Belknap Street in Fort Worth was and is one of the busiest streets in Fort Worth. It is now part of Highway 377 that goes all the way to Denton. We rented half of an old house that backed up to Belknap. We had three rooms and shared the bathroom with the people living in the other three rooms.

The kitchen had no doors on the cabinets. My mother made red and white polka dot curtains to go on the cabinets. They looked cute.

Looking back now, I know the neighborhood was terrible. The big old house next door was a mess and needed lots of paint. Several families lived in that house. There were old rundown small trailer houses parked in front of that house. There was a dirt street beside the house and a 7-Eleven store across the side street.

The trailer closest to us had an older man and his 17-year-old daughter and their two little boys living in it. The little boys were about 1½ and 2½ years old. The mother of the little boys' name was Linda. Linda loved her little boys and did her best to take care of them.

She had a little space beside the trailer fenced in. It was a short fence, but she stayed outside with them when they were outside. When I went to the grocery store, I would bring a little candy back for them. It made the little boys so happy. Social Services came to visit them one day and said they would be back when Linda's father was home. That night, her father hooked the little trailer to his old truck and went away. As I am writing this now, I wonder if my mother called Social Services on them. I don't know. I have often wondered whatever happened to Linda and her two cute little boys.

Two children and their cousin who lived in the other side of the duplex. Linda and her family lived in the trailer in the background.

BELL HELICOPTER

My dad got a job with Bell Helicopter in Hurst, Texas. Bell was moving down from Buffalo, NY. It was his first steady job since we had moved to Fort Worth. Mother went back to work at Convair after some surgery.

We were able to buy some furniture now. The other two

places we had lived in were furnished. I remember looking at a chrome dinette set. They were all the rage then. Everyone had one. The salesman poured lighter fluid on top of the table and lit it. Fire went all over the top of that table. He put the fire out and it was as good as ever. We bought the dinette set! We never had a fire on it again, but no hot dishes or pans ever hurt it either.

I was 10 years old when we moved to this location, and I now was alone when my mother and father were at work. There were no good neighbors here to stay with. Mother and Dad were doing the best that they could do under the circumstances.

With God's help my roots had grown deep to prepare me for times such as these.

GOD'S HAND PROTECTED ME

There was a Peeping Tom who lived in the big old house next to us. With no air conditioning the windows were always open in warm and hot weather.

I would be washing dishes and would hear a cough or sneeze. I would run to the window to see this man running back to his house from our window. This happened almost every night. I guess we did not call the police because we did not want to make him mad at us. I was there alone so much of the time.

Now, it is said that Peeping Toms usually progress to more serious things. We did not have that information then.

I will tell you a little history. Peeping Toms got their names in Covington, England. Lady Godiva was upset with her husband who was the ruler of that area of England. He was going to raise taxes on his subjects who already had a difficult life. He told Lady Godiva that if she would ride a horse through the streets with no clothes on that he would not raise the taxes.

All the people knew this was to happen. They sent word to Lady Godiva that all would put their hands over their eyes and would not see her. All followed this rule except one man named Tom. He and all other peepers from that day forth were called "Peeping Tom."

One summer morning as I was sleeping, I thought I heard someone on the outside of the wall. I looked out the screen by my bed to see a man's face pushed against the screen. That made him about one inch from my bed, which was pushed against the wall. He was a very dirty, homeless man who had decided to put his blankets on the ground by my open window. He was going to be homeless under my window. My mother and dad were at work.

I jumped up, grabbed some clothes I had taken off the night before. I put the clothes on in the bathroom and ran out the front door. I never slowed down until I got to Aunt Lorah's house. She lived about six blocks away. She called the police and they moved him away.

One Saturday my mother and dad had gone to the grocery store. I heard a knock at the door. It was the man delivering our dry-cleaning. I told him that I had no money to pay him and that my parents were gone.

He pulled the screen door from my grip and rushed in. He grabbed me and put me on his lap and started putting his hands all over me. I tried to get loose but could not. I told him he better let me go and get out of there because my mother and dad would be back any minute. I told him my dad would kill him. I kicked and pulled as hard as I could and got away from him. I ran to the door and got on the outside of the screen. I held the screen door open with me on the outside. I told him to get out now. I had decided that if he resisted leaving that I would run to the 7-11 store. I was going to ask them to call the police. He did pretty much run to his truck.

Dad went to the cleaners store location and told them what had happened. Of course, they did not believe that their nice family man employee would do such a thing. Dad told them he would kill the man if he ever came to our house again. He never came back.

Thinking back on this period of my life, I know that God had His hand of protection on me. I did not have a TV and had no idea of the things that could happen to a girl. I was not smart enough to be afraid of all the danger around me.

The best thing about my life while we lived at this duplex was that a man who worked with my dad and his family moved into the other side of the duplex after we had been there for several months. They had a little three-year-old boy and a baby girl. I always loved babies and was happy just playing with these two children. Their mother was a kind woman and appreciated my time keeping the children occupied. I was as happy as could be just taking care of these children.

On Saturday nights my parents and I would go to Aunt Lorah and Uncle JT's house to watch wrestling on TV. We enjoyed it at that time in our lives.

I joined a Brownie troop (young Girl Scouts) while we lived here. I sold a lot of Girl Scout cookies. The problem was that I sold them for 25 cents. They were to be sold at 35 cents a box. This was not one of my best hours. We had to make up the difference. They wore uniforms, but I did not tell my parents because I knew they could not afford to buy a uniform.

My mother made me five gathered skirts while she was off work on sick leave recovering from her surgery. I picked out the fabric and loved my five skirts. We got five shirts to wear with them. On several occasions, girls asked me why I always wore skirts and never wore dresses. I told them that my mother made them and I liked them.

Underneath it all, I knew I was no longer rich but that was all right. I was happy and I could jump rope. I had a baby to play with. What else did I need? Being rich depends on who you compare yourself to.

THE FIRST 3-D MOVIE

One day while my mother was laid off, we walked to Six Points (down Belknap Street) to a movie theatre. We saw the first 3D movie. It was a cowboy movie. I was amazed, but I remember coming out of that well air-conditioned movie theatre into 110-degree temperature. We were not used to air conditioning. Leaving and walking into heat made us both sick by the time we walked back home. It was still a good memory!

The old house we lived in had no insulation, so it was very hot with no fans. I would get a heat rash, which itched a lot. I remember most afternoons running all cold water into the big footed bathtub and just sitting in the cool water.

NOT A PERFECT FAMILY

The worst thing about this time of my life was that I learned that I did not live in the perfect family. It is hard to keep secrets when you live in three rooms. My father wanted to go back to the farm. He did not like working in public works. I heard this many times not knowing what public works was. I guess that means having a boss telling you what to do. My dad did not like that. He wanted a divorce. My mother would tell him that he could not leave us until I was grown. She could not support herself and me by herself.

In my mind, my parents were unhappy because of me. The reason why they stayed together was me. So, my job from that point forward was to do everything possible to make them happy. I walked on eggshells to not upset anyone. In my mind, I know better now, but my heart has always told me I was responsible for everyone's happiness. This follows me to this day. I have, of course, failed miserably at making everyone happy.

Mother was laid off in a big slowdown of Convair. She drew unemployment payments for several months. During this time, she went to a business school in downtown Fort Worth. At the end of this she was well qualified to work in an office.

A SMALL CASTLE

Mother had managed to save a few hundred dollars by hiding it in the Bible. She knew my dad would not find it there. He would have spent it if he had found it.

We went to the south side of Fort Worth to see some brand-new houses. We passed the Southwestern Theological Seminary with a good size Baptist church across the street. It was only five more blocks to the new houses. I knew this was going to change my life. I was so happy I could hardly stay still.

We bought one of these houses and I could walk to church every Sunday. We had not been regularly going to church. My mother had not been well for a long time. I was 11 years old and old enough to walk the five blocks to church by myself, and I did. To me this was one of God's miracles. We had never even been on the south side of Fort Worth.

I do not know how my parents knew about this one street of little houses. It was the perfect place as far as I was concerned. My roots could again start growing deeper.

This castle was small at maybe 500 square feet. It had a big yard. I had my own bedroom. We did not share our small inside bathroom with anyone. There were two small bedrooms, a small living room, a tiny kitchen and a one-stall garage.

A family with a baby girl moved in the house next door. I was happy. This baby ended up being the flower girl at my wedding years later. A girl one year younger than me moved in the house on the other side of our house. We became good friends.

My life centered around the church. All my friends came from that church. They were all children whose fathers were going to the seminary to become ministers. I felt nothing but love from that church! They had a busy youth program. We had recreation (games) on Friday night, services on Wednesday, Sunday morning and evening. After Sunday evening services we had fellowship at different people's houses.

I was in sixth grade when we moved into our little castle. The elementary school went through the sixth grade. The school was at the end of my street. Changing schools is always hard. My friend Alice and I came together at school and church. We were best friends through Rosemont Junior High School and the first year of Paschal High School. Her father finished seminary and moved to a church in Oklahoma. We did visit back and forth after their move. She lived with my family until the end of that school year before moving.

I was baptized at Gambrell Street Baptist Church when I was 12 years old. I came down the aisle to confess my faith in Christ as Lord and Savior. Alice walked with me. I now felt that my teacher Mrs. Williams and older friend Mrs. Ashley were walking with me. My parents were not there, but they were there the Sunday night that I was baptized. I was so happy that my dad did come. As long as I can remember I felt the pull to be in church. I think the Holy Spirit pulled me to be in the church for the support I would need.

HOW GREAT THOU ART

One summer, I went to church camp in Glen Rose. That was the only camp I ever went to. I loved it. The camp was not air conditioned. Texas summers are hot! We had evening worship at night under the sky. The stars were so bright back then with not as much light to drown them out.

"How Great Thou Art" was a famous song at that time. You would hear it on the radio and every place. George Beverly Shea would sing "How Great Though Art" just before Billy Graham came to preach in the Billy Graham Crusades. These were on TV for the world to see.

The camp worship service started and finished with everyone singing "How Great Thou Art." This time for me was a mountaintop spiritual high every night. My roots grew even deeper those nights! I still treasure that song.

EGGS AND BRAINS AND MANGE CURE

Saturday morning was a morning I did not invite any friends to my house. My dad fixed brains and eggs for breakfast on Saturday. Brains and eggs do not smell good at all. It was his favorite breakfast.

My dad somehow got the idea that Mange Cure would make his head grow hair. His hair was getting thin. He had always been handsome and did not want to lose his hair. Mange Cure smells even worse than brains and eggs. It was a good morning to go somewhere else.

VISIT TO GRANDPARENTS

Shortly after we moved to Texas, my grandparents moved from the farm to a house in Okmulgee. Sometimes on Friday night my mother and I would get on a train in Fort Worth and sleep on the train going to Okmulgee. There was a beautiful train station in Okmulgee. It was torn down a few years ago. It made me cry. Mother had come to that train station from Alabama with her mother and two siblings when she was five years old. Mother remembered her father standing there smiling while waiting for them. This was a big move from Appalachian Mountains to Oklahoma.

The Great Depression and Great Dust Bowl hit only a few years later. When we came to Okmulgee, I would stay with my cousin Ida Mae. I loved staying with her. She was a couple years older than me. She was always very kind to me. I was probably an inconvenience to her. I love her still.

ECCLESIASTES 11:1

We always went to my grandparents' house for holidays. I remember one Christmas there we had a house full with some taking turns wearing coats and sitting on the front porch. We heard cries and sobs coming from the house next door. My grandmother told my mother and one of Mother's sisters to go get the woman neighbor and bring her into our bursting-at-the-seams house to eat.

Grandma explained that the neighbor lived in her boyfriend's house. The boyfriend was there a lot of the time, but on Christmas he would be with his wife and children. The wife and children did not know about his girlfriend. The poor woman was alone on Christmas. Grandma said, "Her ways are not my ways, but she needs us." My grandmother always quoted this scripture:

> Throw your bread on the water, because you will find it again after many days. (Ecclesiastes 11:1 GW)

She did not do this to get anything in return. She did this because she loved everyone, and everyone loved her. The neighbor enjoyed eating and visiting with all our family that Christmas.

Some months later, Grandma was having a heart attack in the middle of the night. Grandpa went out on the front porch and screamed at the top of his lungs "Help! Help! Someone Help!" The neighbor lady heard his cry and came running in her robe. She called for an ambulance. She sat beside Grandma's bed waiting for the ambulance. She held Grandma's hand and comforted her as she left this earth and entered heaven. "Throw your bread on the water..."

I will have my own story on this same verse later in my life. Barry's and my holiday table has always been open to anyone without family with whom to celebrate.

APPALACHIAN MOUNTAIN GRANDPARENTS

Everyone in the family thought my grandmother was born in Roaches Cove, Alabama. My grandfather was born there. Working on my ancestry I learned my grandmother was born in Cocke County in the mountains in Tennessee. Even the census in Alabama read that she was born in Tennessee on the Chuckey Knolls River. Barry and I went there and found Talley Hollow Road in Cocke County, Tennessee. Grandma was a Talley. This road is only about 20 miles from where Dolly Parton was born and raised. It was and is one of the poorest counties in Tennessee.

Fifty years ago, where we lived in California, I read a book entitled, *Christy* by Catherine Marshall. It was a true story of her mother coming to a mission outside Del Rio, Tennessee. Around 1900 her mother lived in this mission and taught the mountain children in the first school they ever had. This book was popular 50 years ago to show the poverty and lifestyle of these mountain people.

There was a TV series based on this book, and I think also a movie. A few months ago, I was in a Christian bookstore and saw the 50th year Anniversary Edition of that book. I bought it and reread the book. I was amazed to learn that the mission location of the book is only about 15 miles from Talley Hollow Road where my grandmother was born. To think of what has happened in two generations from my grandmother and me. To think how she lived and how I live today. We live in a great country blessed by God.

My grandmother came to Alabama when she was eight years old. My grandfather's family lived close by. The first marriage between a Talley woman and a Loyd man was a few months later. All the Talley women married all the Loyd men. All cousins were double cousins. My grandparents moved to Oklahoma when my mother was five years old.

My grandmother did not leave her Appalachian Mountain ways in Alabama and Tennessee. When I still lived on the farm in Oklahoma, I got sick probably with a virus. I was never sick, but now I was sick. My grandma's fear was that I had the measles, and I would die if I did not break out with the red spots.

Grandpa drove her a long distance to our farm with her Appalachian cure. The cure was 1 tablespoon of moonshine, 1 tablespoon of coal oil and 1 teaspoon of sugar. She gave me one tablespoon of the concoction. I thought I would never have skin on the inside of my throat again. Since I did not break out and did not die, then I did not have the measles. My grandmother also delivered babies. She delivered some of her grandchildren. I came along after hospitals were the place to have babies.

My grandfather, Ike Loyd, was a large, coarse, mountain man. He worked hard and raised nine children during the Depression. The children worked hard also. They always had food to eat, but not much else. Mother said that every Saturday the kids cleaned the front yard. They even had to pick up all the chicken feathers. Grandpa didn't want anyone calling him "white trash."

My mother said that a man came to the door one day and asked if they could please feed his family. He said he would stay and work for grandpa the next day. This was in the middle of the Depression. They had not eaten for days.

Grandpa hollered for everyone to get into the kitchen. They boiled eggs, cooked bacon, cooked cornbread and pinto beans. Mother said it was the only time she ever saw her father cry. He carried the food out under a tree where the large family sat and ate and ate more. Grandpa came back in the house and sat and sobbed saying he could not imagine having your children hungry and not being able to feed them.

Mother told me of a time when she was in high school that a man knocked on their door. He said that he was taking a truck load of cows to market and one cow had fallen out on the road and died. He told my grandfather that he could have the cow if he wanted. Mother's family did not have beef to eat very often. They had no way to preserve the beef. Pork was smoked in the smokehouse to preserve it. Mother said all the boys worked on cutting this cow into pieces. Grandma and all the girls boiled all the meat in one day. They canned the beef with its juices in canning jars. They had beef soup all winter that year. She said it was a good winter.

An aunt and uncle brought my grandparents from Oklahoma to visit us in Fort Worth. We took them to the zoo. They had never been to the zoo and had never seen many of the animals they saw that day. I still remember Grandma sitting on a bench for such a long time watching the giraffe. She said that she would have never believed that God made such a strange animal. She watched the giraffe and smiled and smiled.

My grandmother died when I was 15 years old. My grandfather died one year later. His coal black hair turned white in that one year. My grandma was 14 years old when they married. Grandpa was 19. Grandma gave birth to 13 children and raised 9 to adulthood.

My grandparents had a hard life. Their first child died at a few months old. They said the little boy suffocated. Who knows? If you slept at grandma's house as a child, you would wake during the night with grandma's hand at the end of your nose. She would be checking to see if you were breathing, if you were still alive.

My grandparents died while we lived in our tiny castle house on Felix Street in Fort Worth. My mother went into a deep depression. I could not make her happy!

FAMILY VISITS IN OKLAHOMA

After my grandparents were gone, we would go back to visit aunts and uncles and cousins. On one trip we were at my cousins Minnette and Huberta's house. Jenney and Ida Mae and I were there. Minnette drove all of us to a natural spring swimming hole to swim and cool off. We were in the pickup. Two were in the front and three were in the back.

All of a sudden, the tailgate fell open and one cousin was out on her bottom on the gravel road scooting down the road. There was a car full of boys who we did not know behind us. I thought they were going to run over her. They stopped just in time and got out to help. They were nice but we told them to go on, we were fine. This cousin would not get up until they left. The bottom of the jean shorts and a lot of her skin was gone. She was to get married the next weekend. She might not want me to tell which cousin it was. That's a picture in my mind I will never forget.

FROM THE COTTON PATCH TO CITY HALL

My mother worked as a secretary in a furniture factory not far from our tiny castle on Felix Street. After some time there she got a job as secretary in the city manager's office in City Hall in downtown

Fort Worth. She had come from the cotton patch to City Hall. She worked hard to get there. She wore nice clothes and high heeled shoes. She loved this job.

At 12 years old, I started cooking the evening meal. I had it on the table when my dad and mom got home every day. I also had a pot of coffee for them to drink. I loved to cook. On Friday after school, I would vacuum, mop and clean the house. I got five dollars a week.

I bought fabric with the money and made most of my clothes. I took sewing for two years at Rosemont Junior High School. I really did love to sew. It served me well. Later in life, I sewed most of my clothes until I was 30 years old. I sewed mine and other people's draperies and other decorating items. I had a drapery shop at one time. Much later in life, I helped my daughter and daughters-in-law to make draperies in their first homes. I helped them make their houses into homes. What fun and what a privilege! What a blessed Mema I have been.

I also loved to babysit. I made 50 cents an hour. One summer a woman behind our house had her first baby and hired me to care for the baby when she went back to work. That was a wonderful summer for me. I also made $15 a week. Sounded like a lot of money to me.

HERBY'S LITTLE SANDWICHES

A friend on Felix Street who had three little girls had a brother who had four little children. She gave them my name to use as a babysitter. Her brother's name was Herby. Their family grew up very poor. The kids often went to bed hungry.

Herby was the oldest of the children. He built himself a small cart to push. He had an area in the cart to hold ice. He would line all the kids up early to form an assembly line to make sandwiches.

He would push the cart and sell sandwiches to the men working outside. He would also sell sandwiches to other workers in buildings which had no eating place close by. Herby was 14 years old when he started selling sandwiches.

Herby's shoe soles would wear out. He put cardboard in the bottom of his shoes to keep from burning his feet on the hot streets. He built this business up and was able to buy a delivery truck. Then he kept buying more delivery trucks.

When I met Herby and his family, he had bought the old Sycamore Schoolhouse and made a beautiful home.

His family was very strong in their Christian faith. He was so thankful for God's help in feeding his brothers and sisters for years. And now the big business is helping him take care of his own family.

Years later when Barry, me and our boys moved back to Texas, the 7-Eleven and other convenience stores sold Herby's Little Sandwiches. These were the first sandwiches sold in this way.

I tried to find the old schoolhouse some years back. There is a street in Fort Worth called Sycamore School Road. It is full of houses and shopping centers. When Herby's family lived in the schoolhouse, it was in the country with not much around. He owned a lot of land around the old school. I am sure the old schoolhouse has been torn down.

Think of what a 14-year-old boy without even good shoes but with love for his family was able to do. He saw a need and he met that need. We live in a wonderful country.

OLD FRIEND – NEW FRIEND

Right after my friend Alice moved from Fort Worth, God supplied me with a new friend. We were in church and Paschal High School together. She had moved a lot because her father was military. She was a good friend to me. I hope I was a good friend to her. Her name was Beverly.

Her father and family were sent to Germany just before our senior year. We wrote letters all the time that year. I convinced her to come to North Texas College with me. She had dated her future husband, Bob, through high school and college. They have been married over 55 years now.

CHAPTER 6

The Love of My Life

I know that God had his hand in all you are about to read. We had moved when I was 16 to a house a little larger. We had two good sized bedrooms, a large living room with a dining room at one end and a large kitchen. The kitchen was large enough to hold the yellow chrome dinette set. It was still just two bedrooms and one stall garage, but large enough for me to have friends to spend the night. It was nice.

I still went to Paschal High School. I could drive to church by then. I never had my own car but we worked it out with one family car.

One hot, hot Saturday afternoon, I was in the garage washing our laundry in the old ringer washing machine. I got a call from Montie, a friend that I went to school and church with. She and her boyfriend, John, wanted to bring a boy over to meet me. John was Barry's friend. I told her to give me 30 minutes to wash and dress. I was a sweaty mess at the time. They came over and we went to the Lone Star Drive-In to get a Coke and visit in the car.

It turns out this boy, Barry, had kept an eye on me for some time. His mother said that he came home one day and told her that he had seen the girl he was going to marry. He told her that this girl had long legs and would give him tall boys to play basketball.

My house had been the first one on his paper route during high school. His family lived one street over and two houses down.

Barry had just finished his first year at Rice University in Houston. He was home for the summer. His friend said that I was too nice and sweet of a girl for him. Barry bribed his friend by loaning his friend his new Johnny Cash record album for two weeks.

We saw each other every day that summer. Of course, it was difficult when he went back to Rice. We both wrote letters every day.

Waxahachie Train Station

Some weekends Barry could come home on the train from Houston. The train went to Waxahachie, then Dallas and then Fort Worth. Barry would call his parents to pick me up and meet the train at the Waxahachie train station. This way he would miss Dallas and we would have three hours more together each way. We would do the same thing on Sunday when he went home.

One day his parents and I arrived in Waxahachie to find that the train was running late because it had hit a cow the day before. It had not made up that time yet. The stationmaster would update on arrival time every hour. Each time the time was moved to a later time. After several hours, the stationmaster ran out and put his ear to the track. He said he could hear it coming. We all ran out to put our ear to the track. We could not hear anything. The stationmaster was back in the station laughing and slapping his hands on his legs saying, "That is my favorite joke."

After being there six hours, the train came. Waxahachie always has had a special place in our hearts. A few times we went to a bed and breakfast there for an anniversary night. That train station was in the movie "Places of the Heart" with Sally Fields. We have watched that movie several times just to see the old train station. What a wonderful movie it was! What a wonderful train station it was and still is.

Barry finished his second year at Rice, and I finished my senior year at Paschal High School. That summer Barry looked into transferring to TCU. That did not seem like a good option. By the end of the summer, we decided we would get married the next summer and I would go to work in Houston to support us for two years while he finished college. Rice has a five-year engineering college. We knew this decision would mean that we would be poor for a long time and we were. We did not want to be apart.

Barry went back to Rice for his third year, and I went to North Texas University for my freshman year.

Christmas of that year, Barry and I got two little boys from a children's home in Fort Worth. We brought them to our house once to get acquainted and then picked them up on Christmas Day. We bought gifts for them instead of each other. It was a wonderful Christmas. When I saw Barry enjoying those little boys, I knew he and I were made for each other.

Barry and me in front of his 1950 Dodge.

HUSBAND AND WIFE

We got married on June 2, 1961. We went to Lake Murray, Oklahoma and stayed in a cabin for three nights. It was $15 a night. We could only afford three nights. On the way to Lake Murray there was a man on the side of the road with a little baby. He had a flat tire. We stopped to help him. He was on the way to his parents' home to leave the baby with them. His wife was in the hospital. We drove him and baby into the next town so he could call his parents to come for him. I held the baby. She spit up all over my going away dress. My mother said she thought I could go on my honeymoon without a baby messing up my dress. If there was a baby around, I would always find it, hold it and get my clothes messed up. It happened even on my going away dress.

We came back to Fort Worth and loaded everything we owned on our little 1950 Dodge and went to Houston. Neither one of us had a job, but we were happy as could be. We bought a watermelon from a farmer on the way to Houston. There was no room for it in the car. I held it in my lap the rest of the trip. I love watermelon.

I got a job at Houston Natural Gas in downtown Houston. I could ride the bus there. Barry got a job at a large commercial construction company for the summer. I made $225 a month. We lived off of that by eating hot dogs and cheap hamburger and lived in cheap places in terrible areas of town. We did not feel unsafe because drugs and the crime that came with drugs were not a problem at that time. The good Lord took care of us because we were too dumb to even be aware of bad things that could have happened to us. We didn't have a phone. We would save change to go to a pay phone to call our parents. We mostly corresponded by writing letters.

We thought that this was a wonderful life. We did think that this was to be this way just until Barry graduated. It did not change greatly for a few years.

Our wedding on June 2, 1961 in Fort Worth, Texas.

OUR FIRST BIG STORM

On Labor Day weekend, Barry's parents came to visit with us. We lived in a tiny very old garage apartment. His parents slept in the bed and we slept in the back of their station wagon. There was not enough floor space to sleep on the floor in the apartment. Hurricane Carla was coming onto land. The wind blew so hard that night that I thought the station wagon and the two of us were going airborne. The next morning at daylight, Barry's parents were there with suitcases in hand telling us that they were going to Fort Worth. We could go with them if we wanted or get out of the station wagon. They had spent a lot of time during the night listening to the radio about this hurricane.

We spent the next night on the floor of a school gym. We were without electricity for about a month. The house in front put an extension cord from there to our window. We plugged the refrigerator and one light in it. We would sit in our one chair by that light for a month. We did not have much to plug in anyway. We didn't own a TV and the microwave had not been invented. We never had air conditioning while in Houston. We thought life was good anyway.

HOUSTON, WE HAVE IS A PROBLEM

The first January we were married and living in Houston a very cold spell came in. It is very unusual to get below freezing in Houston. The door locks on our car froze up because of the moisture in the door and we could not get into the car. We managed to unlock the trunk, crawled through the trunk and pushed the back seat down to get into the car.

At this time, we were living in a three-room duplex in a very old house. The house was on blocks and had the water pipes running up outside walls. To keep the pipes from freezing we turned the water faucets on to run slowly and fixed the toilet so it would continuously run water. The cold air came up through cracks in the flooring into the living areas. There was on old fashioned space heater with a gas line coming from the walls. This heater was the only source of heat for the three rooms and the bath. We bought some plastic to put on the floor and covered it with many layers of newspaper. We then covered the newspaper with old blankets. We closed off the doors to the other rooms. Needless to say, we were glad to see the cold spell move out!

CHAPTER 7

Making a Family

We decided that we wanted to have a baby before Barry finished at Rice. We wanted this baby to be four months old at graduation time so we could travel to wherever we moved for his job. We counted back and decided when we needed to start that baby. It all worked like a charm. That baby was four months old when Barry graduated. It never quite worked that way with our other babies.

Barry had $2,000 in U.S. Savings Bonds when we got married. These were saved from when he was a kid doing various jobs such as mowing his grandparents' yard in Pennsylvania. That would be enough to take the place of my income until he started his job.

I knew company policy was that I could only work until I was five months pregnant. That was the way it was back then. That all worked out fine except our car fell apart. We borrowed $500 to buy a 1955 Ford. We just had to show the offer for the job at IBM to get the loan. That was all we owed when he graduated except for a washing machine we bought after the baby was born. Barry didn't like to take the baby into the laundromat. He was afraid the people in the laundromat might inflict the baby with something. We lived in a really bad part of Houston.

Our first wonderful child was born on February 9. We named him Curtis. Curtis is Barry's middle name. We were so excited with this bundle of joy. He was just what we both wanted so badly. "Puff the Magic Dragon" was a popular song played on the radio at that time. Barry would rock Curtis and sing that song. As Curtis got old enough, he would start smiling and laughing as soon as Barry started singing that song. We knew that God had blessed us dearly. Even in the hardest times we have always known that.

Barry, me, Curtis, my mother Irene, and father Everett Howard.

OFF TO KENTUCKY

Barry's job was at IBM in Lexington, Kentucky. We settled in the small town in Georgetown a few miles north of Lexington. We did not know a single person in Kentucky. God watched out for us always.

I soon ventured out knocking on doors to find a friend. The only other child on the street lived in the house across the street. The mother was in her 30s and had her first child. The mother was a nurse and had married late in life for those times. It was good to know a nurse! She was lonely being at home after working in the hospital for so many years. I was lonely home alone knowing no one and not even having a TV. We visited every day while we lived there.

The heat did not work in this house. That was why there were signs that the last people living there had burned coal in the fireplace to stay warm. It gets very cold in Kentucky. We moved to a little house one street over so that we would have working heat. It was a very small two-bedroom house. Georgetown was a small town. Most of the people living there had all their family there and families had lived there for generations.

We went to church the first Sunday we were there. I started teaching the two-year-old Sunday school class! I met my new friend Joyce there. She had a little boy just a little older than Curtis. Her husband had grown up in Georgetown, but she had moved there her senior year of high school. After she was married her family moved back to Indiana. We became the go-to friend for each other. We kept each other's boys for our doctors' appointments, etc. She was the friend God gave me there in Georgetown.

I didn't have a car when Barry was at work. Joyce and I could walk the six blocks to visit. Finally, I was able to buy a stroller which made the walk easier. We could always walk downtown. Town was stores on both sides of the road for two blocks. Curtis enjoyed going in the stroller. I was as happy as could be.

Me and Curtis by our 1955 Ford in Georgetown, Kentucky.

FIRST THANKSGIVING IN KENTUCKY

We were lonely and decided at the last minute to join family for Thanksgiving in Franklin, Pennsylvania. Barry's two grandmothers and his Uncle Jim and family lived in that area. Grandma Kockler lived with Uncle Jim and his family. Barry's family still lived in Fort Worth. They moved back to Pennsylvania a few months after Thanksgiving.

We didn't tell anyone we were coming. Curtis was nine months old. It started snowing really hard after we were on our way. It was 4:00 in the morning just a few miles from Uncle Jim's house and our car broke down. We coasted into a gas station just as the car stopped totally.

There was no pay phone outside, and the station was closed. It was too cold to stay there in the car with no heat. I did not know about real cold, cold weather at that time. We did have a snow suit on Curtis and a couple baby blankets for him. We decided to start walking to town. I opened my car door to have a huge dog run toward me. He was growling and showing his teeth and barking at me. I got the door closed very quickly. I got out the driver's side. The dog was chained to a gas pump and could not reach that side of the car. After a short time, a deer hunter stopped for us. I had never gotten in a car with a stranger before, but I had never been that cold before.

The hunter took us downtown to a hotel in Titusville to use their phone. Uncle Jim was surprised to hear where we were. He came to get us. He knew someone who repaired cars at his house close to where our car broke down. Anyway, they got the car fixed. We had a nice Thanksgiving and came home on Sunday. After that, I was always more prepared for cold when we took a trip north in the winter.

READY FOR ANOTHER CHILD

I was an only child. I was so afraid of Curtis being an only child that I was anxious to have a second child. Keith was born a little early. When we came home from the hospital, he weighed 4 pounds, 8 ounces and was 21 inches long. He was very thin. He woke to eat every two hours. He would get too tired to eat much. The doctor said I should feed him as often as he wished. I was breastfeeding him, so I was the only one to feed him. There was not much sleep for me. Curtis was 19 months old and very busy. We did make it through this time. At three months old Keith weighed 13 pounds which was the same as Curtis weighed at three months old.

Barry's mom came to help me when Keith and I came home from the hospital. She took one look at Keith and said, "He is not the kind of baby you want to invite the neighbors in to see." She had no filter and said what she thought. He became a beautiful baby in no time at all.

Barry was studying for his master's degree oral exams at the University of Kentucky during those times. Barry was also a Boy

Scout leader for the church scout troop. It was a sleepless, busy time but we were so proud and thankful for the addition to our family.

GOD GAVE US MORE FRIENDS

There was a couple, Paul and Rosalee, who moved into part of the house across the street from us. They were expecting a baby also. Paul was going to college at Georgetown Baptist College. They had a little girl 10 days after Keith was born. Neither family had any money to do much, so we played cards most Saturday nights. We could put all three kids to bed and enjoy playing a card game called Rook. We had fun.

I had an Avon lady come every month. She was such a pleasant woman, and we became friends. She was older than me, but we enjoyed visiting. She had a high school aged daughter. When Barry had to go out of town on business or Scout camps, she would stay with me. I taught her how to sew during those times. We made her some cute things to wear. She also enjoyed the boys. I was so thankful for their friendship.

There was another older lady who lived down the street who would come for most days for an hour or so and play with the boys and would visit with me. Also, it gave me a chance to gather clothes from the clothes lines in the back yard while she played with the boys. I did not have a dryer.

A WONDERFUL LIFE WITH LITTLE MONEY

After five years at Rice, Barry only made $700 a month. We did manage to buy me a sewing machine and TV. I had $20 a week to buy groceries. I fixed a $1 meal every other day. The kids always loved those $1 meals the most. We would have scalloped potatoes with spam on top, pinto beans and cornbread, macaroni and hamburger goulash or sloppy joes.

On Sunday nights, we all together fixed a Chef Boyardee pizza with hot dogs sliced on top. We would eat this meal in front of the TV watching "Bonanza". That was a big treat for all of us. All these meals fed all four of us for less than $1 a night. We had a wonderful life!

AVON LADY

I decided to sell Avon to make money to buy some furniture. I paid the older lady down the street to come while the boys took their naps.

There was no such thing as credit cards. It was not as easy to get in trouble with debt. We could borrow money for the furniture. If you did not pay the payment each month, they came and got your furniture. We bought a couch and rocking chair with two side tables for the living room, a bed, chest, a dresser and two nightstands for Barry and me. The payment was $80 every month for a year. By selling Avon I managed to make the payment and the money for the babysitter and a little extra for income taxes.

I was also able to meet some young women my age in their homes while doing this. It was hard to knock on people's doors and introduce yourself and try to sell them something. After I got to know the ladies in my territory, I enjoyed seeing them and they seemed to enjoy visiting with me.

I was so proud of our first new furniture. We had lived the first five years of our marriage with very old unmatched furniture from Goodwill. I always have loved decorating a home. I have never been as proud of any furniture as I was that furniture that we bought with my Avon earnings. I remember getting up in the middle of the night just to go in and look at it. I wanted to make sure that it had not been a dream.

My mother and father got a divorce while I was pregnant with Keith. I thought they would do this as soon as I left home. I know it was scary for both of them. They were such different people and had been unhappy for so long. I loved them both. They both remarried great people and were happier. Dad did not go back to the farm as he always said he wanted to do. He retired from Bell Helicopter at 63 years old.

One day I was delivering Avon and the lady told me that her son had chicken pox. Of course, I had not had chicken pox. No one at Evening Star School had chicken pox. A few days later, I became very sick. Chicken pox in an adult is quite different than in a child.

Barry was at work and the boys had to be taken care of. I had no family there. I remember feeling the walls going down the hall to the kitchen. I would black out when I stood up, but the boys had to be fed. About the time I got well the boys came down with the chicken pox. By the time we were all well, a month had passed. It was a difficult month.

MORE FUN TIMES

Of course, the favorite time each year was Vacation Bible School. I taught every year for over thirty years. I loved every year of it.

One other fun thing we did was pack everything and the boys up and go to the drive-in theater. I would pop a big grocery paper bag full of popcorn. We would fill a red and white gallon Thermos with Kool-Aid. We put the potty chair in the back. We had a Rambler Station Wagon by this time. We put down quilts and blankets in the back. There were always two movies each night. At that time, all movies were what we now call "G" rated. Barry and I always hoped the boys would go to sleep after the first one. It usually did not happen. But it was a fun time for $1 a carload.

My friend Joyce and I would take our boys to a park on a creek close to downtown Georgetown. She had two boys also by this time. We each pulled a wagon full of boys and food for a picnic. I always made frosting with cocoa, butter and powdered sugar. Put that between two graham crackers and you have a treat for the tummy of little boys.

One of these wagon trip picnics was on the first warm sunny days of spring. We laid out everything and all of a sudden realized these big rocks were moving along the edges and under the blankets. We stood up and realized that the rocks had snakes along all the edges warming themselves in the bright sun. You have never in your life seen two ladies get four boys, blankets and food in wagons and up the hill to the street so fast. We all got out with no injuries. I don't know if we hurt any snakes. I didn't look back to check.

The house we lived in had a basement which had a large empty space where the boys rode tricycles. They were told to not ride between the washing machine and heating unit.

One day they were there playing, and riding tricycles and Keith came up crying with bubbles coming out his mouth and nose. The truth came out that he was riding where he was not supposed to be and knocked over the washing detergent. He decided to eat the evidence to avoid getting into trouble.

The new thing in washing detergents was to have bleach crystals in the detergent powder. I always had the poison emergency number close by. This was not my first time to need that number. I called and was told to use powder mustard to make him throw up. I had that in the cabinet.

The more he threw up in the toilet and I flushed, the more soap bubbles came up. We were above our ankles in bubbles on the bathroom floor. It takes a lot of mopping to get that many bubbles up. I can say that the floor had probably not been that clean before that day.

IBM where Barry worked had lots of organizations for the workers. We took square dancing lessons. We loved doing this. The club met about every two weeks in a school gym. The kids all came along and played together on the sides of the gym floor. It was a good time for all of us.

OH, BUT TO OWN A HOME

We enjoyed our five years in Georgetown. We had been married for seven years and were ready to buy a home. There were not many homes for sale in Georgetown. We found a new subdivision about 17 miles from Georgetown outside of Versailles, Kentucky. We had a home built there. It had a large yard. It was a split level with three bedrooms and one bath on the top level. The kitchen and small living room were on the middle level. The lowest level under the bedrooms was one good size den/playroom and a utility room combined with a half bath.

The neighborhood had kids for the boys to play with. They had never had kids living close to our house. As usual, God had a friend waiting for me, Louise. She lived a few houses down from our house. Louise's youngest was a boy between Curtis and Keith's age. They had so much fun.

The church was on the square downtown Versailles. There was a Methodist Children's home between our house and the downtown. It was started, I believe, just after the Civil War to take care of all the orphans. It was several two-story buildings on many beautiful acres. Kindergarten was not in public schools at that time. The home ran a kindergarten to prepare their children residents for school. They opened for outside children also. This is where Curtis went to kindergarten. He loved it.

TIME FOR THE DRY MUSTARD AGAIN

Barry's mom and dad had come down for a visit. They had been back in Pennsylvania for about four years at this time. We were sitting outside with them when a little girl from the next street came over and walked around us for a few minutes as the adults talked. When there was a let up in the conversation, she said in a matter-of-fact way, "Keith is going to die." I said, "Why do you say that?" She went on to explain that she had sprayed bug spray on some candy and gave it to Keith. She had then asked her brother who was older about what would happen if someone ate the bug spray. He told her that they would die. She said that she just thought that she should tell us that Keith was going to die.

Barry went to get the spray can while I got the poison emergency number. We called and gave Keith water with dry mustard in it. Thankfully, Keith did not die. He did live. He threw up the poisoned candy.

HONG KONG FLU

On Christmas Day, I was bending down to get the turkey out of the oven and suddenly felt very sick and dizzy. I managed to make it through the day without anyone knowing. My mother and her husband were with us. My cousin and his wife and little toddler were with us. My cousin Sammy was stationed in Kentucky with the Army.

Mother and Roy left the next morning. Roy went to the hospital as soon as he got home. From World War II, Roy had only part of one lung. This was the Hong Kong Flu epidemic.

Roy had code blue two or three times and was brought back to life. By the time it was all over in our family, we all had it. Thank goodness we all lived, but it was not easy.

CHANGES ARE COMING

Barry and I had always wanted a big family. Now that we had a little larger house and a nice play yard, we decided it was time for the next baby. After I got pregnant Barry saw an opportunity to get into his own business. This was his dream.

Barry's father had put in a metal treating business in Pennsylvania. They saw a need for one in the South.

It was hard for me to give up the first home we owned. We only got to live there for a year. Also, I was pregnant and would have to move in mid pregnancy, find a doctor in a place where I knew not a soul and knew no doctor. We would have to take the money from the house to put in the business. We would rent someone else's house again.

I kept praying, "God, how can I do this? I have to do this. You have to work it out. I need a miracle from you, God." We decided the business was going to be in Statesville, North Carolina.

We put a "For Sale by Owner" sign in the front yard. Within a week a young couple came. They loved our house and wanted to buy it. She asked where we were going to move. I told her Statesville, North Carolina. She said "That is where I grew up. All my family still lives there." I told her that I was pregnant and would be having the baby there in October. She said, "I have a cousin there who is pregnant and is due in October. She has two girls now." She gave me her cousin's name and phone number. She said she would talk to her cousin and she would be waiting for my call.

Curtis was still in his kindergarten year and would not finish until the end of May. That was about six weeks after we were scheduled to give possession of the house to the new owners.

The doorbell rang. A man told me he was running for County Judge. He wanted me to vote for him. I told him I would be glad to vote for him, but I had sold my house and needed a place to live until my son finished kindergarten. I told him that I would not be able to vote for him unless I found a place to live for six weeks. He said he and his family lived in Versailles in an old Victorian house they bought the year before. They were fixing it up.

A lady lived in three rooms downstairs and she would be moving soon. Her brother was the present county judge whom he was running against. She had never let him into the part she lived in. Therefore, he had never seen that area of the house.

We had a moving company pack up and store all we had except what we needed for that six weeks.

I cleaned and cleaned those three rooms for us to move in. There was a big hole in the kitchen floor. When the lights were off at night, rats would come up from the basement and eat our dog's food. I patched the hole. The heat didn't work well. There was a cold front that came into town. We found something to put on the floor to protect it and used the toaster oven to help with the heat.

It was a beautiful, large, Victorian house. The people had fixed their side downstairs and the upstairs, and it was so nice. They planned to fix these three rooms to match the rest of the house. They were just waiting for the current renter to move out and then we came along. We were grateful the man had knocked on our door asking for our vote. We could do this for six weeks. We wanted Curtis to be able to finish kindergarten.

The owner did win the election. They were nice people and really nice to us. They had a beautiful Irish Setter that could jump high enough to keep all birds from flying over the yard. He would jump up and grab every bird in the air.

I was having a cup of tea with the lady of the house at their kitchen table. One of their three boys came in. The Irish Setter came leaping through the door and up across the kitchen table and through the living room and out the front door. The dog's feet hit the floor only three times to get through the house and out the front door. Our cups of tea were broken to pieces and were on the floor. They had three little boys and that dog. It was an active household.

Our two boys played well with their three boys. There were huge trees in the back yard. The five boys were in the trees all the time. The week we were leaving Curtis fell from a high limb. He said he jumped. Whichever it was, his elbow was broken requiring surgery and a cast.

We loaded up a rented trailer and the boys and off we went for Statesville, North Carolina. Barry had gotten lots of good work experience at IBM. He was one of the first to work on the Selectric typewriter. It had a ball with all the letters on the ball. You could change balls to change typestyles. When it came out, it was considered the best. This, of course, was before computers. Everyone used typewriters.

IBM also paid for Barry's master's degree at the University of Kentucky. He also had paid time off to go to classes. He was ready to try something different. He wanted to have his own business.

THE MOTEL WITH A POOL

I called the cousins of the new owner of our house. She was Carol and he was Michael. They were very nice and welcoming to us. They had beautiful little girls our boys loved playing with. Carol and my delivery dates were just a few days apart.

Carol and Michael had us over to eat the second night we were there. They were truly a gift from God. They showed us a house under construction four doors down from them. They knew that the man was building the house for his rent house. He was building it himself around his regular job. He said he would let us move in it as soon as he could finish the inside. He could brick, etc., after we moved in.

Carol said that her girls were starting Vacation Bible School the next day. She offered to pick my boys up on her way the next morning. The boys were excited. I was really excited. About one hour after they got to the church, I received a call to come to pick up the boys because they were broken out with the measles. They had been fine when they left the motel. My friend Louise in Kentucky had us over to eat at her house the night before we started to Statesville. The next morning all three of her kids had the measles. I did not know this until Curtis and Keith came down with the measles.

We could not swim because of the cast on Curtis's arm. Now we could not eat out at an air-conditioned restaurant. We had to eat in the car or bring food into the motel room. The car also did not have air conditioning. It is hot in the summer in North Carolina.

THE HALF-BUILT RENTAL

We moved into the little house. There was a drop cord with a plug. That was the only electricity we had at first. We ran extension cords to the refrigerator and to floor lamps in all the rooms.

The moving company came with, I thought, our furniture. The man stopped in and asked which room I wanted the furniture. I said I thought the couch, etc. should go in the living room. They should put the bedroom furniture in the bedroom and the kitchen table in the kitchen. The moving man said, "Ma'am, I only have a baby grand piano, a China cabinet and a large dining room table." I could have sat in the floor and cried, but that would not have helped. I asked him to please find our furniture as soon as possible. None of what he had was ours.

The next day, I broke out with the measles. No one at Evening Star School ever had the German measles so I had not had them. I went to see the OB/GYN referred by Carol. He said I was five months pregnant and it should not be a problem. German measles is very dangerous for the baby in the first three to four months. Sometimes the baby would be born blind and/or dead. I became unable to bend my fingers and ankles. The doctor said that is what happens to pregnant women who get measles in the last three to four months of pregnancy. That lasted about two weeks.

We did get our correct furniture in a couple of days. But I had to heat water on the kitchen stove and take it to the bathroom for baths. The hot water had been hooked up and was working. The city inspector came and disconnected the hot waterpower because the hot water heater was not vented through the roof. It was in a small space at the end of the one stall carport. That space had not been framed nor bricked yet. It was sitting in the wide-open spaces at the end of the carport, but it had to be vented through the roof. Therefore, I had to heat water on the stove to wash dishes and for baths, etc. This is all difficult when your fingers do not bend.

Curtis's elbow healed nicely. We had to take him to Charlotte to a doctor for that. Ticks were a real problem in the red soil in that area. We took him to the doctor in Charlotte. The doctor took the cast off. Under the cast was the fattest tick I had ever seen. I had no way of knowing the tick was in there until they took the cast off. My life was so full of surprises.

There were lots of really sweet children in that neighborhood. All ages played together every day. Curtis and Keith had a really good summer. The father of the children behind our house had been out of a job for months. Back then you made do because there were no food stamps, etc.

They bought 50-pound bags of flour, oatmeal, cornmeal and dried pinto beans. The family had homemade biscuits and oatmeal for breakfast. At lunch they had beans and cornbread. At night they had some vegetables grown in the garden to go with their beans and cornbread.

These kids loved to eat lunch at our house. We had white bought bread and lunchmeat. Curtis and Keith loved to eat lunch at their house. They had beans and cornbread. So, all summer they ate every other day's lunch at our house and the other day at the neighbor's house.

The father of this family who had been out of work worked for Barry when he got the plating business going. Also, Michael started selling the plating once the business was up and running. Do you see how all these pieces fell together? God had His hand in there making all these pieces fit together just right. It wasn't the parting of the Red Sea, but it was the miracle we needed at that time and in that place. People from little Statesville, North Carolina came to our door to buy our house. And all these parts came together from that. Don't you see God's fingerprints?

Carol delivered her third baby girl and a week later I delivered my third baby boy in October. Carol and I had fun with all our kids.

Curtis spent the first grade in Statesville and enjoyed school.

A HAPPY BABY – A NEW LIFE

Steve was a happy baby and healthy. There were no problems from the measles. I was so relieved once he was born. I was told there should not be problems, but it is always in the back of your mind. Praise God for helping me through this whole year of upheaval.

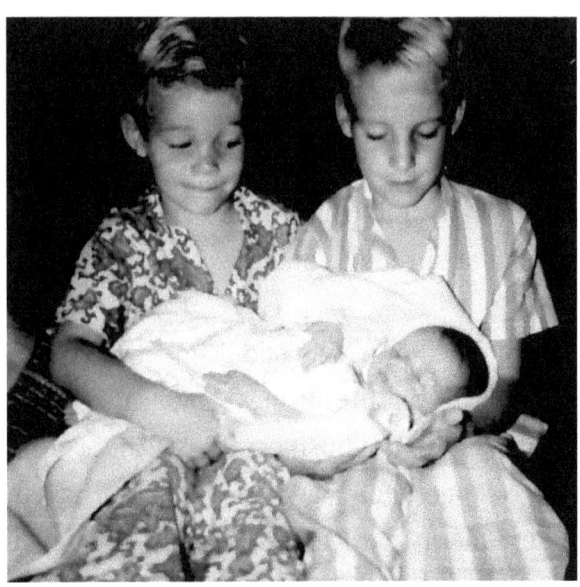

New baby Steve with brothers Keith and Curtis in Statesville, North Carolina.

As we settled into our new life, we were very content. It seemed life had smoothed out at last. Unfortunately, this would not last long. When Steve was three months old, we learned that Barry's father had lung cancer and had not long to live. He died six weeks later. He was 52 years old.

Barry's dad was a good man. He was a good father and a wonderful grandfather. He died too young. He had smoked from a young age. He got lung cancer because of that. He lost so many years of life because of this smoking and we lost more years to enjoy him. Grandchildren, please do not smoke anything other than hamburgers on the grill. It will hurt your lungs!!

We do not grieve as others who have no hope according to the Bible. Bob Kockler had a great faith in the Lord. We will see him someday in heaven.

Barry's father was part owner of the business. After his death, we decided that it was best to sell the plating business. There was a man in Pennsylvania who desired to buy the plating business from us and to combine it with a machine shop he would operate. He continued to employ the men who were working there – our friends and neighbors.

CHAPTER 8

Time for Another Plan

When one door closes, you find a window to go through. We decided it was best for Barry to get back into engineering. He decided he wanted to work for a smaller company after six years at IBM. The Statesville area did not offer that opportunity.

We bought some newspapers from areas we thought might work. Barry answered an ad in Greeley, Colorado for a start-up company. This company was building a product that added a paper tape punch and reader to the IBM Selectric. Barry, Steve, and I flew to Greeley to look around. Friends kept Curtis and Keith at home. Barry applied for and got the job. We cried as we left Statesville.

We found a house to buy in Greeley. It was being built and we could pick our flooring, etc. It was going to be six weeks to move-in time. We found a motel with a small kitchen and two rooms. That was easier than one motel room.

I prayed, "Oh, God, bring me a friend." The second weekend we were there a man from the company invited us to eat Saturday night with his family. They cooked hamburgers and had homemade ice cream. Ray and his wife Jean were a little older than us and had three girls ranging from 14 years to 9 years old. They had just moved to Greeley from Boulder to work for the new company. They were a strong Christian family. They were the friends God sent for us in Greeley. We had so much fun together and today, 50 years later, we are still the best of friends. We have taken so many trips together. We had lots of motorhome trips together. Thank God for just the right friends for Greeley and for always.

Curtis started to second grade and Keith started first grade while we were in the motel. I drove them there each morning. Once we got in our house, they could walk to school. There were several kids in the neighborhood to walk with them.

All was good so I started to make draw draperies for the big windows in the house. I was learning and Jean was my teacher. I missed Statesville but loved being in our house again.

We did find a church we loved. It had a wonderful children's program. We were not close but were closer to Fort Worth and my family. Greeley was a nice size town. We thought we were settled. I had just put the last hem in the last drape when Barry came home early to tell me the new company had been bought by a large company in California. Barry looked for a job in Colorado, but it was a slow time for hiring engineers there, so we were off to California.

MOTEL LIVING IN CALIFORNIA

We always preferred to keep the family together in our moves. Some wives and kids stayed put until homes were sold and the next home ready to move into. That was fine but was not for us. We loaded up and were off together for California.

We looked for a smaller town that could be in commute distance for work in Cupertino. We found Scotts Valley up in the mountains in the redwoods. The population was 5,000. There was one motel which consisted of about 12 old cabins in a U shape. They had a little kitchen with two beds and a couch. They were very old but clean. Now we knew where to look for a house and knew where the boys would go to school. There was a doctor's office, a drugstore and a grocery store. Now all we needed was a house to make into our home and a church.

I prayed that old familiar prayer, "God, bring me a friend once again." We found our home. It was on the far side of a mountain down a small gravel road called Cadillac Drive, just about three miles up the mountain from town. It was small but fairly new. We had three bedrooms and 1½ baths and it sat on two acres of redwoods.

There was almost no flat area except for the top of the driveway. The drive was almost straight up and long. Curtis and Keith were upset because they were worried about how they could shovel snow off that much driveway. We told them that we had left all the snow in Colorado. They felt better. The hill was so steep that it was planted with ice plant rather than grass.

We had to wait six weeks to move into the house so present owners could find their next house. Curtis and Keith started school. Soon a family from South Carolina moved into the motel. They had a high school boy and two girls a little older than my boys.

They were a wonderful, strong Christian family. The mother Doris and I had everything in common. We both loved to sew. They were warm southern people. And guess what? They were waiting to move into their house on the same road as our house. From our house, you could only see two houses. One of these houses was the house this family was moving into. Do I have an awesome God or what? Doris was my new friend God had sent for me once again. This was a miracle that God worked for our family in California.

The day we moved into our house I was excited to start putting it all together and decorating it into our home. Barry was at work, of course. He was working with the same engineers he had worked with in Greeley. Not much had changed in his world.

The moving men came to the door to inform me that the big moving truck could not make the left turn to drive up the steep driveway. Their plan was to unload everything at the bottom of the driveway. We would have to get it all up the driveway and into the house.

I told them not to unload one thing at the bottom of that driveway. I called Barry and told him that unless he was going to carry everything up on his back that he needed to do something fast. He went to the relocation manager. After lots of back and forth the moving company agreed to send up a small moving truck. Everything was reloaded one load at a time onto the small truck and up the driveway and into the house. It took many, many trips and it took forever. I am sure it cost somebody lots of money. We did not have to pay for it. What a stressful day… at the end a happy day!

WE SETTLED IN ONCE AGAIN

We found a wonderful church. Again, it had a great children's program. The next summer, I taught Bible School there. There was a mother's club that met once a week as a prayer group.

Doris and I did lots of sewing together. I had gone with Jean in Greeley to a tailoring class. I actually made Barry a sports coat while in California.

Blackberries, acacia trees, and blue bellies grew wild on our mountain. Doris and I made loads of blackberry jam, cobblers, etc. The kids all loved helping us pick the blackberries.

There were lots of blue belly lizards on our property. Steve was two years old and loved helping his brothers find blue bellies. He would come running and yelling "Boo bellies!" with one in each hand. He called Keith by his name but could not say Curtis, so he called him Keith II. Curtis did not like this at all, but he was nice to his little brother anyway.

There were beautiful acacia trees mixed in with many redwood trees. The acacia trees were covered with beautiful yellow flowers. I loved them at first. Curtis became very sick. He was so, so allergic to these trees. I had to rush him into the doctor's office one day. They gave him an adrenalin shot. He turned white as a sheet and could not breathe. Everyone in the office was in there working on him for a long time. I was so scared. They brought him out of it and we went home. I thanked God, but I never thought again that those trees were so beautiful.

There was a deck across the front of our house looking down the mountain. Early fog would roll in from the ocean each morning. We would look out on top of the clouds before it lifted on up and over our house. We were above the clouds and then we would be in the clouds for a short time. The plants loved the fog each morning. Only time that I had a green thumb was with the help of the fog.

DEN MOTHER IN A UNIFORM

As a child, I never got the Brownie Girl Scout uniform. I became a Cub Scout den mother, and I had a den mother dress and hat. I had about eight boys in the den. Curtis and Keith were both in this Cub Scout den.

We did lots of cool things and I loved doing it. We went to a special location which was a stopping place for the annual monarch butterfly migration. There were butterflies everywhere. They were landing all over us. I could not imagine so many huge butterflies in one place. I probably enjoyed it more than the boys did. Of course,

Steve went everywhere with us. It was his favorite day of the week when all those boys came to our house.

OKIES ARE FEARED

Our closest neighbor was across the street from our house. She had never been out of California. Her father and her husband were both college professors. She and her family had just moved from the city into their house about three months earlier. She had heard that the people moving in across the road were from Texas or Oklahoma. She was actually very scared that our kids would give her kids lice and would be very dirty kids.

During the Dust Bowl and the depression, people from Oklahoma and Texas farms lost everything they had. They heard that California would have jobs. They loaded their families on the big farm trucks and came to California. The jobs were not there for them. They ended up living in their trucks and tents going anywhere they heard of work. These were hardworking farm people just trying to take care of their families. They had no access to bathrooms and were not able to stay clean. They sometimes lived in labor camps that were crowded and they did get lice.

The people of California did not like the Okies, as they called them, and my neighbor did not want to live close to Okies. After the depression the Okies were able to get jobs and support themselves. This highly educated woman who had never been out of California thought people coming from Texas and Oklahoma would still be like the ones who came during the depression.

We did not know how this neighbor thought and we made this situation worse within two days of moving in. There was a very large tree close to the road beside the driveway. Barry put up a tire swing on a limb of this tree. The boys could swing off the far side of the driveway for a nice long swing. It was the best tire swing ever. The boys were having a ball on it. We were not living in the city by any imagination. We were on a gravel road in a very wooded area. Curtis and Keith would help Steve to enjoy the tire swing by putting him on their lap. The neighbor was horrified at first.

My neighbor lady did finally meet me and my Okie family. She was surprised that we were clean, well-educated people. Her children loved playing on the tire swing with my children and they did not even get lice from us. When we did move, she told me that it had been enlightening to have met us. That is when she told me what she had thought when we moved in. She also told me to never change, that she liked me just the way I was. I always try to make friends with everyone, but sometimes it is harder than other times. But I am glad I kept at it with her and we became friends. Maybe God put me there for her sake. I don't know!

The boys were on baseball teams. They enjoyed that. Every long weekend or holiday we went to explore all the beautiful parks and Disneyland. We made it a good life, but we did not feel like it was home. It was the most beautiful place that we had lived, but it seemed like we were on vacation, not at home. It was the first place where we had felt that way.

Barry received an offer to work in Boulder, Colorado. It was a start-up company. He went to check it out and decided that he would like the work. It was November and not the best time of year to move, but that is what we did. It rains in California in November. It was pouring rain when we left.

BACK TO COLORADO WE WENT

We left on Friday night and Barry was to be at work in Boulder on Monday morning. I don't know why he agreed to that timetable.

Doris's son was a senior in high school. We paid him to drive one car pulling a dune buggy while Barry drove one car pulling a pop-up camper.

We got to the Sierra Mountains, and, of course, it was icy and snowing. That is when I thought that this young man driving the car I was in had lived in Florida and South Carolina and California. He had never driven in ice and snow. He had never seen ice and snow on the roads. We stopped and I told Barry that I was not happy. I put all the boys in the car with Barry. If we skidded over the mountain, at least Barry and the boys would live. I also thought in the darkest part of my mind that if that happened that Barry deserved to have to raise three boys by himself. He should not have agreed to start work in Boulder on Monday.

He stopped for a few hours to rest in a motel. I had been wetting towels in ice water to put on the young driver's face to keep him awake on the winding snow-covered roads.

We did get to Boulder on Sunday night. The friends from Greeley (Jean and Ray) had moved from Greeley to Boulder when we went to California. We stayed with them. Barry took our young driver to the airport. We paid for his ticket home. We found a motel to live in and Barry went to work.

BOULDER WIND

We found our house right away because we had to know where to enroll Curtis and Keith in school. The people selling the house had to have six weeks to find another house and move out.

One evening we went to the laundromat to wash clothes. Thank goodness Barry was able to go with us. There was ice partially melted just enough to be very slippery. We came out to go to the car with two baskets of neatly folded clothes. Some of Barry's new dress shirts were on top of one basket.

The Chinook winds had come out of the mountains while we were inside. This is common in Boulder to have these very hard winds. I opened the door and Steve went out. I followed with the basket of folded clothes that included Barry's new dress shirts. The wind started pushing Steve very fast on the wet ice. He was standing flat footed but was being pushed very fast toward the busy road.

I set down my basket and ran to grab Steve. As I did this, the wind started to suck up the shirts one by one from the basket. The shirts filled with the wind with arms straight out and flew straight up. The shirts were flying up just like a kite. I looked up to see four shirts flying in a row going up and a little to the east. They went up until out of sight. We got in the car to try to catch up with them. We, of course, were not able to see them anymore. They were still going up as they went out of our sight. Some people were probably surprised the next morning to find men's shirts in their yard. I hope they fit them.

LIFE IN BOULDER

Every place we lived I found wonderful people, and this was true in Boulder also. But the most difficult person I had ever run into was next door to our house in Boulder. He was a man in his late 50s and lived with his 19-year-old girlfriend. The girlfriend's family lived behind our back yard. The man was heavy and wore a bikini under his belly with a BB pistol stuck in the bikini. He was a professor at the college. From the time I first saw him and tried to introduce myself, it was clear that he did not like me and was not going to speak to me.

If the boys played kick ball and the ball crossed onto his driveway he would run out and get the ball and take it inside. The boys would ask him for the ball, and he would say they could never have it back. If I rang the doorbell he would not answer.

There was a gate in the back of our fence. The girlfriend's siblings would use the gate to cut through our yard to go see their sister. They were friendly and visited with us if we were outside. Sometimes they forgot to latch the gate. Our dog would get out when this happened. The dog would go into the front yard of the professor. When this happened, he would shoot our dog with the BB gun he always had with him.

The professor had a cat who came over his tall back yard fence to use Steve's large sandbox every day. I always had to go clean it out before Steve and his little neighbor friend could play in the sandbox.

Grandchildren, please listen. There are some with whom you cannot reason. He was doing nothing illegal. I tried to take homemade cookies over as a peace offering. He would not answer the door and would never talk to me. I did pray for him. He must have been a miserable man. How sad for him. We just had to put a lock on the gate to keep the dog from being hurt by him.

The younger siblings of the girlfriend finally told me what made him hate us. Turns out that the day the moving van was unloading into our house, Steve and his newfound friend had peed into the basement window wells of the professor. It seemed easier to them than to try to get into the bathroom around moving people. Also, those three-year-old boys probably thought that they liked that solution better.

Sometimes you have to take what comes at you in life and make the best of this life as you can. You must also learn from your experiences. Today we live on 1½ acres. If a neighbor hates us, at least we have some distance between us.

There was a Methodist Church behind our house and one street over. We loved this church. They had a ladies Bible study which I joined.

That summer I headed up the Vacation Bible School. It was not as hard of a job in that size church. It was fun and we brought in a lot of unchurched children from the neighborhood to learn about Jesus.

LIKE NONE OTHER

It turns out that Barry's job with a start-up company required him to work 12-hour days seven days a week. It was the first time ever that the boys had no daddy around, and he could not go to church with us.

We had really wanted to get back to Colorado, but this was what we had dreamed of. We couldn't ever get a day to go to the mountains to enjoy being in Colorado.

During the summer, word came to Barry that the start-up company was being bought by a larger company. Everyone was going to be moved to California.

At the same time this move to California news came, Barry heard that the company he worked for in California was being bought by Xerox and moving to Dallas, Texas. These people would be the same people he worked with in Greely, Colorado and in California. The head man was happy to have Barry work with them in Texas. Sometimes my whole body felt like it had whiplash.

They flew us down to Dallas to check it out. We knew we would not want to live in the big city. Xerox was moving to North Dallas very close to 35E. We drove north on 35E and found the little town of Lewisville. This was just what we wanted. Lewisville had a population of about 6,000 at that time. Barry got a good job offer. We went back to Colorado to pack up and move to Texas.

CHAPTER 9

Back to Where We Started

We had been married in Fort Worth 12 years earlier. My dad and his wife lived in Fort Worth. My mother and her husband lived in Oklahoma City. They were all very happy to have us closer. It was like coming back home. It had just fallen into our hands. I now know God had His hands in the whole thing. Don't you see God's fingerprints?

We found Double Oak where we still live 48 years later. We have 1½ acres. There were only 5 or 6 houses completed and with people living in them in Double Oak. Lots of other homes were under construction. We found a slab on a lot with two very old large post oak trees in the back yard. There were five other trees on one side of the front yard. I loved the one very gnarled and very old tree in the back. I told Barry I wanted that tree, and I was sure the house would be good. Later we met with the builder and it turned out that I loved the house also.

You get more house for your money in Texas. This house would be twice as large as our largest house up to that time. We would have three bathrooms and they were all inside and we did not have to share them with another family.

Lewisville only had three elementary schools, two middle schools and one high school. We started Curtis and Keith in the third and fifth grade at Central Elementary. Of course, we were again in a motel. It took two months for the house to be finished for us to move in.

Keith, Steve and Barry all had birthdays in the motel. The dream was for this to be our last move, but of course, we did not know. Leaving friends when moving is so hard for everyone. I hated that Curtis and Keith had a new school every year. Barry felt like he would be able to find work in this area even if this job did not work out or moved away.

We found First Methodist Church right away while in the motel. It was a small church with a lot of friendly good people. My whiplashed body started to heal.

On November 1, 1973 we moved into our wonderful home. I had for the first time been able to pick out what went into our house. Oh, but Lord, I prayed, "I need a good friend here."

MY NEW GOOD FRIEND – "THANK YOU, LORD"

I spent a couple of long days unpacking. I went outside and looked around. An empty lot was across the street. The street curved and facing that street with the side of the house toward us had life in and around it. I got a two-liter Diet Dr. Pepper in one hand and Steve in the other hand. We walked toward where we saw life. I rang the doorbell. A sweet small pretty lady with a smile on her face and a mop in her hand came to the door. I said, "I am Prue Kockler, and this is Steve. I need a friend and you must be that friend. I just moved in across the street around the curve." We had a Diet Dr.

Pepper and visited and visited more. I knew that I had struck a gold mine with my new friend, Judy Markland.

Within a week, Judy and I were in a car together on our way to Denton for a Bible Study Fellowship class. Oh, Dear God, you really did well! Don't you see God's fingerprints?

Bless the Lord Oh My Soul

Bless the Lord oh my soul
Worship His holy name
Sing like never before
Oh my Soul like never before
Oh, my Soul I'll worship your holy name.
The sun comes up
It's a new day dawning!!!

Judy had a daughter a few years older than Curtis. She had a son between Curtis and Keith's age. She had a nine-month-old son who came to worship Steve. They all had lots of fun together. Judy's husband Jon and both our families became the best of friends.

Judy and Jon and Barry and I still get together as often as we can even though they were sent back to Indiana after a few years. We are still best of friends and talk often and take trips together when we can. Thank you, Lord, for answered prayers! No one has ever had a better friend than Judy.

Steve and Joel Markland.

Keith, Jim Markland, and Curtis.

THINGS WERE GOOD IN TEXAS

Curtis and Keith came back from the first day of school to report that they needed different clothes. Everyone wore western shirts and jeans. There was a western wear store on 35E Interstate and Main Street. We went that evening and purchased proper school clothes. They looked so cute.

Friday nights were Lewisville Farmer football game nights. Everyone in town went to the game. You could not buy even a loaf of bread on Friday night. There were no chain stores. Just stores locally owned. They closed for football night.

We went as a family. To sit in the reserved section, we put our name on a long waiting list for season tickets. You had to wait for some season ticket owners to die.

The big old station wagon I drove had no air conditioning. I went at night to buy groceries, so nothing melted in the hot weather.

We put in a large garden at the back of the yard. After many years, we gave up on the garden because the water bill was so big. It did give us many years of good vegetables.

Within three weeks Barry, the boys and Jon Markland had a treehouse in the back yard. Soon we got a swing hanging in that beautiful old, gnarled tree.

A lot of our life happened under that old tree. Most Easters we have pictures of the family dressed in Easter clothes in the swing under our old oak tree.

There is an old song that Jimmy Dean recorded.

I just thank God for His blessing and the mercies He's bestowed
I'm drinking from my saucer 'cause my cup has overflowed.

I truly felt my cup had overflowed with God's blessings and mercies.

There was a skating rink on 407 about four miles from our house. There was not anything else on 407 at that time. Curtis and Keith would often go skating on Saturday nights. It was the place to be. They always had friends there.

Curtis and Keith joined the Boy Scout troop at our church. Barry did a lot of the campouts with the troop. I remember there was a survival camp they did. They were pretty worried about it. Then I found out that the survival camp part was just for four hours. They had nothing to eat except what they could find for four hours. I think they were surprised that they survived.

For the first time in our life, we had central heat and air. That was lots of luxury to me. Barry had said when we first talked of moving back to Texas that he planned to have a pool. The first Good Friday we lived here we worked on rotor tilling the front yard and putting grass out. We were so hot and tired by the end of the day.

Barry said that we needed to get a pool to fill some of that big back yard. He did not want to plant grass that would be dug up for a pool.

We started that process. We paid monthly payments of $116.00 for six years. In six years, the pool would be paid for as Curtis started to College. I had never dreamed of being able to have a pool. I was scared of spending that money. It was probably the best thing we did. Our kids' friends were usually here to swim. We knew their friends. That was such a blessing.

There were always lots of kids here and we loved it. Barry was right! We needed a pool. Now grandkids are here in that pool a lot and we love it!

The day the pool was filling up with water there were a line of kids in bathing suits with towels in hand watching at the sliding door. No one was supposed to go in the pool until the water was on the tile. Just as that happened a big storm came in. So sad.

There was one winter day I was not sure about the pool. It was very cold, and some pipe froze that kept the water from circulating. The top of the water froze to more than half an inch thick. There was a danger that the tiles could break. We told the three boys to put some breaks in the ice. I was folding clothes and watching out the sliding door as they were using baseball bats to break the ice. I saw Steve lay down on the slide with his face hanging off the side and start to hit the ice. I ran out to get him off just as he hit the ice with the bat and knocked a hole in the ice. It was a hole big enough for his body to fit through.

Of course, as the bat hit the ice it made a hole in the ice. His little body went through the hole and he was under solid ice. Just as I got there Curtis had gotten his hand in the hole and grabbed Steve's hand and pulled him back to the hole so he could pull him out. I grabbed Steve and ran to the bathtub to get water on him to warm him up. To this day Steve says I ran all hot water on him. It was all cold water. I knew I needed to warm him slowly. I know it felt like hot water to him. We were all scared. When one has a bunch of kids you can't let your guard down.

Thank the Lord they all lived to adulthood. Now all I can do is pray each day for God to watch over them, and I do that each day!

Gnarled oak tree with swing and treehouse.

Family picture in 1974.

SNAKES, MICE, AND STINGING SCORPIONS

The first time I opened the dishwasher in this new house, I saw two mice running on the bottom of the dishwasher. No one believed me. How could mice get in a sealed dishwasher?

I did not feel like my dishes were clean. I rewashed them in the sink by hand. I tried the dishwasher again. I saw mice again and I now had proof. There were mice droppings in the bottom of the dishwasher!

I bought mouse traps and put them in the bottom of the dishwasher with cheese in them. I caught a mouse the first night. I took pictures to show people who thought I was crazy. I continued to do this each night. I caught four mice in four nights. I continued for several nights to put the loaded trap in the dishwasher until I was sure that we had no more mice.

I don't know how the mice got into the dishwasher before we moved in. They lived in the insulation and ate the scraps of food and had water to drink. They had their own little ecosystem going.

I also had stinging scorpions in my bathtub each morning when I got up. Their stings do not kill you, but they sure do hurt for about 24 hours. I had put on gardening gloves off the picnic table one morning. A scorpion was inside. It stung me two times by the time I got the gloves off. The plumber found a broken sewer line right outside the wall by the bathtub. They fixed the pipe, and that problem was over.

We did sometimes find snakes in the house. It turns out that Copper Canyon Township across 407 was not named for a copper mine. It was named for its abundance of Copperhead snakes.

I kept shovels and hoes and other snake killing instruments at several places around the house. This land had always been wild and farming land. We do still have a snake to kill from time to time.

The last snake a few months ago was on the front porch. Barry had been sitting on the front porch for a while before going to bed. He had been working on his iPad. I heard him holler to me to bring something to kill a snake. He was holding it behind its head with the edge of his iPad. All I could find in the kitchen where I was that could kill a snake was a pizza cutter. You would not believe how tough the skin of a Copperhead is. I did cut the head off finally. As we always told the kids, you must be careful killing a Copperhead. The mouth will still bite you if you get a finger or whatever near its mouth even though the head is cut off. By the way, I threw the pizza cutter away.

The boys with large rattlesnake killed on a dove hunt.

Everett and Gioneth with our family.

Grandpa Howard and Steve on the swing.

THE MARKLANDS LEAVE

Sadly after a few years the Marklands had to move back to Indiana. Jon tried to find a new job here, but that did not work out. They liked living here, but we do what we have to do.

Judy and I talk every week or two and we get together here or there or someplace in between as often as possible. Health problems that come and go make it more difficult to get together now.

I gave Judy a plaque that said, "Heaven is perfect. Therefore, I know that we will again be neighbors in Heaven."

OUR FAMILY WAS NOT COMPLETE

After settling in and staying a few years in Double Oak we started talking about the other child we had planned to have. We always wanted a large family. Time was slipping by. At that time doctors told us not to have children after the mother was 35 years old. I know that has changed.

Most people either have their children earlier in life or in later life. It is not financially advisable to have them both early and late and some in between. One thing I really do love about Barry is that his decisions are not based around financially wise decisions. He does consider that, but he thinks with his heart also. Pleasure that results in a decision sometimes outweighs the dollars and cents. He did say that this would delay retirement but that was fine with him. We became very excited about having another child. I wanted my kids to have lots of siblings and I wanted my grandchildren to have lots of cousins. I wanted big crowds on holidays like I had at my grandparents' little house.

We made the decision, but everything took longer than we had thought it would. I finally did get pregnant but sadly I lost the baby at about two months. I was getting closer and closer to 35 years. I did get pregnant again and all went fine. I think everyone thought we were crazy or that this was an accident. Some thought that we were just trying for a girl. I had not even considered that to be an option. We just knew that we were having another sweet little boy and that was just fine with us.

I was excited to decorate a nursery. With the babies before, we never had a nursery to decorate. I went and picked out wallpaper for both a boy and for a girl (just in case). I prepared the walls for wallpaper. Before I came home from the hospital, I gave Barry the wallpaper information to order and pick up.

We were all very shocked and excited when Tammy was born. Barry had said that he was getting older and would do better at watching dance recitals and piano recitals rather than teaching baseball, etc. to another boy.

The day Tammy was born Barry was sitting in my hospital room holding her. He said to me, "Wouldn't it be fun to have another little girl to play with this one?" I quickly told him that I was too old, and our family was complete. He would have to wait for grandchildren.

Tammy was awake a lot the first night we came home. We just stayed up all night wallpapering her room. It looked so cute. It was fun to do a room girly.

Curtis was 15½ years old. Keith was 14 and Steve was 9 years old. They had fun with Tammy. When she was a little older, they would sit her on a blanket and pull her all over the house. She loved it and she loved her brothers.

Tammy on her first Easter.

ADDING A ROOM IN THE HEAT

We wanted to have a pool table for the boys. They could have friends over to play pool. We added a large room onto the end of the kitchen eating area, which also opened to the kitchen. The old TV room with sliding door to the pool became the pool room and Steve's bedroom for the time being. Steve thought that was great.

We paid for the slab to be poured and we started to work with our hammer and saws. Just as we started to do the framing Barry had wrist surgery and could not use a hammer. This was before nail guns. The boys and I nailed every nail by hand into those framing boards. We were new at this and used lots of nails because we bent so many nails.

The year 1980 held the record for many years as the hottest summer on record in Texas. That was the year we added the new room onto our house. Barry, Curtis and Keith put the roof on. The tools would become too hot to pick up. They burned their hands. They would start at 7:00 in the morning and work until 11:00. They would start again at 6:00 and work a couple of hours. In the middle of the day the temperatures would get up to 110 to 112 degrees. That is hot.

The pool room got a lot of use with young people playing pool. After all the kids were grown, it became Barry's office. He has used it to run his business for many years. The pool table was donated to the church youth group. It took lots of large boys to move it.

Tammy helping add the room.

Keith helping frame the new room.

THE SUPPER CLUB GROUP

A few friends talked about forming a once-a-month get-together group to eat and fellowship. We decided 12 people or six couples would be just the right size. We all knew a couple or two to add to our group. None of us knew all the couples.

We all knew we wanted Christian couples who had traits in common. We all agree to this day that this has been such a blessing to all of us. We all wanted a casual down to earth club. We decided to call this The Supper Club. We have shared our lives for over 35 years.

All of our children were still at home when we started this group. Now we all have grandchildren, and some have great grandchildren.

We had one couple move away after a few years. We added another couple to replace them. We have been the support for each other during the best of times and the worst of times. We have all been there to help bury all of our parents. We have been there to celebrate the birth of grandchildren and even to bury one grandchild. We have been there for all the weddings. We have done the wedding showers and the grandbaby showers. We have all gathered to put hands on and to pray together when the diagnosis was cancer. Two of the men in our group have died. We all are so thankful for all the years we had with them. We loved them to their last breath. One of their wives has remarried. We have welcomed this wonderful Christian man into our group.

Everyone is amazed that we have had a group of 12 people for over 35 years and there have been no divorces. We have never met that we did not have prayer together. I encourage my grandchildren to find a group of Christian people with whom you can share your life – the good and the bad.

We also traveled lots of trips with this group. We went on an Alaskan cruise, Caribbean cruise, to Branson and flew to Atlanta to visit the couple who had moved away from our group. We have lived a lot of life with this precious group of friends. I know God brought us together. God uses us on earth to be His hands. We have been God's hands for each other.

The Supper Club in 2019.

HELPING START A NEW CHURCH

We had been at First Methodist Church for some years when the opportunity came to help start a new church in Flower Mound. There had been great growth in the Flower Mound area.

Six couples, including us, met in one of the homes. All the couples were from First Methodist. We all knew each other. Mr. & Mrs. Trietsch had donated land from their farm for a new church. The Trietsch family still had an egg farm and hand delivered eggs to homes at that time. They were not a wealthy family but had a large farm in the middle of Flower Mound on Morriss Road. At that time Morriss Road was two lanes of a mixture of gravel and some paved road.

A retired Air Force chaplain was going to be our minister. He had a good retirement income so his family could live on that and our modest salary. The Methodist Conference also helped with beginning expenses.

We all worked hard for about two months before we had our first service at the cafeteria of Timbercreek Elementary School. We had about 100 that first Sunday. The adults at first thought it to be strange to listen to the sermon delivered under a big tiger head. It seemed normal to the children.

It took all of us to pull off church on Sundays in this cafeteria. Each Sunday everyone who had them brought porta cribs and playpens for the nursery. We set up Sunday School children's classes in the classrooms close to the cafeteria. Someone loaded chairs from another's barn on a big flatbed truck. Others unloaded chairs and made a church out of a cafeteria. After church this was all done in reverse. And then some of us mopped all the floors where we had used them.

The youth group met on Sunday nights at people's houses. The middle school youth met at our house. Barry and I came up with the program each Sunday night.

The adult Sunday school classes met at other members' houses. If you were in this church, you had a job and you also felt very needed. It was a lot of work for everyone, but we all knew where to get the strength to do all this. Prayers went up from all of us every day to make this work.

I took Tammy a month or so later to Timbecreek Elementary to enroll her in kindergarten. She said, "I did not know that I was going to school in a church."

Our first Vacation Bible School was at Chinn Chapel Church. At that time there was just the one small white 100-year-old building that made Chinn Chapel Church. Each of we teachers had a tree to meet under. We nailed a sign showing the grade of our class on our tree. There was no air conditioning, and the two outhouses were the bathrooms. Outhouses were a new experience for most of the kids and also most adults there. The opening with singing and the closing each day was inside the white chapel.

I had an older retired schoolteacher come to talk to my class about growing up in this area and about how much the churches meant to the first settlers. This lady was from the Morriss family. Morriss Road is named for her family. She told the kids about the revivals held by each church every year. She said that everyone went to all the revival meetings of all the churches. It was a special time for all the farm kids all around. She said that it was a spiritual and fun time for all of them.

One day I took my class across the road to Chinn Chapel Cemetery. We did tombstone rubbings and I told them about some of the people in the graves. I told them the first church was there and was a log building. Then it was used as a school. We were using a school for our church, but the first settlers built churches that were later used also as a school. Our country was built by Christians who served God. God has blessed our country.

The Trietsch Family was a pioneering family. Mrs. Trietsch was born a McGee by where the McGee store is on highway 407. They donated the land for the church. When Mr. and Mrs. Trietsch were young, they had bought their 100-acre farm for $10,000. Mr. Trietsch once told of a time during the depression that he almost lost the farm because he did not have the money to pay the taxes. They had grown up going to the country church revivals. Their faith was strong.

Trietsch Memorial Methodist Church is a large church now. Mr. & Mrs. Trietsch are dead now. Houses sat on their old farm. We no longer attend church there, but we did for over 20 years. The church is still there and growing. Barry and I are so thankful for the blessing of helping plant that church.

SHELTER FOR STRANGERS

We went to Oklahoma City in February every year for my mother's birthday. As we headed south for the trip home one year, we ran into a terrific ice storm. All of the semi-trucks on Interstate-35 had become stuck in the ice.

When evening came the temperature dropped and the trucks could not move. All the cars, including ours, were stuck between the trucks. This started in Oklahoma and continued south of Dallas. We could not keep the heat on in the car or we would run out of gas. It was extremely cold! There was an older couple in the car in front of us travelling to their son's house. The wife recently had open heart surgery.

After a while, Barry and some of the men from other cars got out of their cars to start pushing and half carrying the cars to the grass. This moved them to the access road which allowed them to move with no trouble. One by one the cars were on the access road! Each freed driver came back to get the other cars out. The elderly couple in front of us ended up following us home. They spent the night with us because all the motels were full. I cooked breakfast for them the next morning before they headed off to see their children.

CHAPTER 10

Venture Adventures

Barry always said he did not live for his work. He worked to support his family. Do you see why I love him so much?

I never wanted a big career. Of course, when you have children there is always need for more money. I had several part-time businesses that I worked out of our house. I am so thankful that I was able to do things that I really enjoyed while making some extra money.

I had a custom drapery business. I had other people to make the draperies. I went to people's homes with samples. I helped them make their house into a home. I also had a custom picture framing business in our garage.

I did craft shows in a big way. My daughter-in-law and I did dried flower arrangements and other decorating items for craft shows. One Christmas season of shows I made enough to build the two-story storage barn for our back yard.

I made ruffled curtains with six times the fullness of the ruffles. I bought a special sewing machine to make the ruffles. One summer I did enough window coverings to buy the three boys some bonds to use for college.

One big thing I did for four years was run a pita bread sandwich business. I went into work this from 10:00 to 2:00. I had some lovely friends from church who carpooled in and worked four hours each weekday. Curtis and Keith and their friends from church youth group worked at night and cut all the meat for the next day. We had a room in back for Tammy's playroom. She was two years old when I started this sandwich shop. There was a lady's fitness gym next door to us. I joined that gym because they allowed me to bring Tammy over during the one-hour big rush. She enjoyed playing with the other children in the childcare section.

The young people worked the Saturdays. Barry and I went to help on Saturdays during Christmas shopping. We were next to Toys 'R Us. Christmas season was big. Prestonwood Baptist Church at that time was down Arapaho Road from us. They paid us to use the shop on Sunday mornings for a Sunday school classroom. We sold the business when it was time for Tammy to start to the first grade. I needed to be home for the school bus. After sandwiches I worked part-time in antiques for many years.

The Pocket Place sandwich shop in Dallas.

BARRY'S FAMILY BUSINESS VENTURES

I say "family business ventures" because work always affects the family. Barry worked on product development at various companies until he was 60 years old. His first job after college was in product development at IBM in Lexington, Kentucky. At IBM, he was one of the first to work on the Selectric typewriter. The Selectric typewriters had letters on a ball that could be changed to obtain different typestyles. This was before computers were common. You now find Selectric typewriters in antique stores.

In 1983 Xerox was being sent to California. We had done that once. We decided to stay where we were. No more moving!!! Barry and Roger Gray, an electrical engineer who had worked with him for several years at Xerox, started a corporation called Devtek Development Corp.

The company did engineer consulting including product development work for a wide variety of clients. Sometimes their business load required them to hire as many as 20 people to work. They built a building to house this business. Later in life, some of the spaces were rented out for income. Even later, we sold the building which helped our retirement.

A big economic slowdown came. The first thing businesses do is drop all consulting jobs. We needed to figure out something else. Barry and Roger had worked together all those 15 years and we are all still the best of friends. Roger and his wife Connie are part of our Supper Club. You could never ask for a better business partner nor for better friends.

During all those years of product development, Barry was awarded 36 US patents. The various companies that he worked for have rights to the patents as this is considered a normal part of product development work.

Barry and Roger in front of the Devtek building.

ANOTHER ONE OF THOSE MIRACLES

We were thinking what now? We prayed what now? We knew that we were not ready for retirement. Barry was 60 years old. Tammy was still in college. She had been dating Jeff since they were in high school. We knew they would marry soon. We thought we might sell the house and downsize. We loved our house and we still do but felt we should check into this option.

I had seen in a local paper the name of a realtor who lived in Double Oak. I did not know him, nor did I know anyone who knew him. He came to our house to tell us what our house should sell for. He looked at us and said, "Do you really want to move?" We said, "Not really."

He had noticed a certificate hanging over Barry's desk from Texas Professional Engineering. He explained that he had been a professional engineer in the state from which he moved. That is why he noticed the little 8x10 certificate on the wall. He said that he would have to work in Texas under another registered engineer for six years to be able to be a Texas Professional Engineer.

This realtor told us that Barry should just go into the foundation engineering business. He said it is hard to find one when selling a house where the foundation has problems. He had seen our motor home in our back yard. He said he could just arrange jobs around trips. We had no idea there was such a job out there. Barry got college books on soil and such from Rice University. He studied up and prepared himself for this new venture. At Rice he studied for four years in various branches of engineering. The fifth year he specialized in mechanical engineering. This had well prepared him for a variety of jobs. I had asked God, "What now? He needs a job." Who knew that a realtor who had been a professional engineer in another state would be the realtor we would call? God did! Don't you see God's fingerprints again?

There probably would not be another realtor in the state with his background. This was the answer to our prayer. This was a miracle for us. No one could have asked for a better post-retirement and part-time retirement job. Barry will soon be 80 years old and he still does a few jobs a month.

At first, we sent hundreds of letters to realtors in the DFW metroplex. Jobs came in by the hundreds. We worked really hard at this business for several years. It did so well that we were able to do some things to the house we had wanted to do. We put in a water well and a sprinkler system and many other improvements.

I answered the phone all day and sometimes into the night to make appointments. After Tammy and Jeff had their first child, Tammy quit teaching. She and Grant would come here three of four days a week to help do the reports on the computer. I answered the phone and took care of Grant. She could make money and I could play with Grant. God is so good!

Barry has done over 6,000 foundation reports. He has not run any ads in six years and now people still call him. They will say, "You did my father's house" or sometimes now they may say, "You did my grandfather's foundation." Barry says it still makes him feel like he is helping someone.

Foundation engineering has proven to be a great semi-retirement job. Barry still goes out on a few foundation jobs each month. This allows him to get out and meet new people. He enjoys it. We are so thankful that God laid this opportunity in our lap.

TRAVEL AND FUN WITH THE KIDS

We wanted to show our kids God's beautiful creation and as much of the landscape and history of this country as we could. It is important to know our history to know what other people have gone through for us to have our freedom and a good life.

We were so silly that we took Curtis to the Houston Zoo when he was three weeks old. After Keith was born when we were in Kentucky, we got a tent and started taking them to state parks and anyplace we could set up a tent.

When the boys got a little older, we took them and our tent to the Smoky Mountains anytime we had some days off. The Smoky Mountains are my favorite place to spend time. I always felt like I was home when I was there. At that time, I did not know that my ancestors on both sides of my family had come from there.

When we were about to leave North Carolina, we took the boys to Myrtle Beach. We were moving to Colorado and we had not taken them to a beach to see the Atlantic Ocean. Colorado was in the middle of the country. Little did we know that a little over a year we would be living on the west coast within 20 miles of the Pacific Ocean.

While we were in North Carolina we bought a pop-up camper. It was handmade by someone and very old. That is what we could afford, and we did have lots of good times camping in it and using it as we moved to new locations.

When we moved we found fun things to see. On the way from Colorado to California we visited Yellowstone National Park. I remember studying in grade school about Yellowstone. I couldn't believe that I was seeing it in person.

In California we took advantage of every long weekend to take the three boys to see the state. We went to Disneyland and later to the big redwood trees that you could drive the car through. We also took them to Yosemite National Park. We really had lots of fun together.

After we moved to Texas, we all went to Galveston every year on a long weekend. Some people said that Galveston was not that good of a beach. It was close enough and cheap enough and we enjoyed it every year. We thought it was great!

The first summer we were in Texas we camped on the Buffalo River in Arkansas. We rented canoes to go down the river. Curtis was in my canoe. Barry, Keith, and Steve were in another canoe. Curtis was ten years old and Keith was eight years old.

The river was low because it had been a dry summer. We would have to get out and carry the canoe in some places. The rocks were slippery as could be and we all fell many times. We had cut up knees. Keith and I were not good at steering the canoe. We went from one bank to the other bank. This added lots of miles to our canoe trip. One time we were headed for a tree limb hanging off the bank. I looked up and looked straight into the eyes of a large snake hanging off the limb. I still don't know how, but I got that canoe going the other direction in no time at all.

One summer we got to the Grand Canyon. None of us had seen it before. That same trip we saw Carlsbad Caverns. Steve was running to our pop-up camper and fell face forward onto cactus. His face was full of cactus spears. The spears were very fine, but there were hundreds of them stuck in his face. Thankfully, they missed his eyes. Barry spent a long time pulling these out of his face with tweezers. Both Barry and Steve were very brave. I was not that brave.

Each year we went back to Pennsylvania to see Barry's family. We also sent his mother airplane tickets to come to see us sometimes. We sometimes took trips in that area with his mother after we got there. She enjoyed that also.

The family situation was different. His mother married her brother-in-law after her sister died. Barry's uncle became his stepdad and the uncle's daughter who had been his cousin became his stepsister. I told you it was a different situation.

Barry's cousin (stepsister) was raising a darling daughter by herself. The mother had health issues, so the little girl was not able to travel much. She was our Annie. She was a couple years younger than Tammy. We all became very close to her. She was so cute and sweet; how could you not love her? One summer we took grandma and her husband (Uncle Frank) and Annie to Amish country for several days. It was such a fun trip for all of us.

Another trip we took was to Niagara Falls. About four years ago, 13 of our family members all flew to Pennsylvania and visited with Barry's brother and family. Many who had not been there were able to see where Barry lived for the first 12 years of his life. That's when we took a two-day trip to Niagara Falls. Some good memories.

Kockler's and Lilly's visit Niagara Falls - Back row: Jeff Lilly, Creed's head, Tammy Lilly, Stacey Kockler, Steve Kockler. Middle row: Grant Lilly, Makayla Kockler, Gabriel Kockler, Prue Kockler, Barry Kockler. Front row: Charlotte Lilly, Hannah Kockler, Clark Lilly.

The first money I made from my custom drapery business was spent on a new pop-up camper. It was nice and we wore it out over many years of camping with the kids all over the country. I am so thankful that we were able to do so much when the kids were growing up. I hope they have good memories. I do!!!

Bears were present in many of our trips. When Curtis and Keith were young, we camped in the Smokies in a tent. Of course, bears were always around. No one took food into the tent because the bears would come in to get it. Barry always kept a hatchet under his pillow. I would wake up with Barry having the hatchet in his hand saying, "Shhh, there's a bear." Usually, it was leaves blowing around. Sometimes this happened many times in one night.

One evening in the Smokies we were cooking Jiffy Pop popcorn on the open fire. There was a big bear on the mountain. The wind was blowing the popcorn smell up the mountain. The bear kept moving a little at a time down the mountain toward us. By the time the popcorn was popped the bear was down the mountain and coming across the road toward us. Barry put the popcorn in the open trash can and we all ran into the car. We watched through the windows as the bear enjoyed our popcorn. Then, the bear went back up the mountain.

Barry, Steve, Tammy and I were in a log cabin outside of Jackson Hole, Wyoming. Barry's and my bed had no headboard. Our heads were against the log wall. We woke up feeling something rubbing against the logs on the outside of the cabin. Then we started hearing bear noises. There were no locks on the front door, nor the back door. They just fit kind of loose hanging in the door opening. We did not want this bear inside the cabin with us. Barry got up and said he would take care of it. He came back to bed. I said, "What did you do?" He explained that he stacked empty Coke cans against the inside of both doors. I asked him how will that stop the bear. He explained we would hear the bear come in and we could run out the other door. Somehow, I could not relax and go back to sleep. The next day we saw where the bear had mashed all the plants against the other side of the wall. Thankfully the bear did not come inside our cabin.

Barry and the boys would go dove hunting on Labor Day. It was a big day with lots of good memories for them.

Barry and the three boys went deer hunting after Thanksgiving dinner for many years. They would be in such a hurry to get through eating so they could go hunting. They would eat in a hurry and leave. There I sat with all that turkey and all the other food and a kitchen full of dirty dishes. It was a special time for father and sons. They would come home in a few days and be starved and would eat all the Thanksgiving leftovers.

UPGRADE TO A MOTOR HOME

I had always dreamed of having a motor home. Barry was not that sure about a motor home. Our friends, the Ellises in Colorado, got a motor home and invited us to go with them on a motor home trip. Barry drove it while we were on the road. He said I was right. We need a motor home.

We had 16 years of wonderful memories of different trips in the motor home. There is a learning curve to doing motor home trips. Our first trip we took my mother back to Florida where she and I had lived during World War II. She had never been back to that area. She was unable to travel any other way. The bed and couch in the motor home were perfect for her. She really did enjoy the trip. We did have one problem along the way. There was a wind as we went across a bridge in Alabama. The awning came loose and opened to the side. We had to stop on the bridge and close it back. That was a scare. From then on, we put a Velcro strap around it to keep that from ever happening again.

One of our first trips in the motor home we were going down the highway. Honking of a horn started behind us. Barry could not think of why a car behind us was honking. Finally, he told me to go look behind and see what was the matter with that car. I came back to tell him that it was our tow car that was honking. The key was in his pocket and somehow, he had punched the alarm button on the car key.

Another time we met our friends, the Marklands, in Branson, Missouri. We went into town to eat. There was a huge hailstorm while we were gone. On our return we heard our little Yorkshire barking and sounding very scared. The bedroom slide-out was going in and out and beeping as it did. As soon as it was out, it went right back to beeping all the time. Water had soaked the circuit board that controlled the slideout motor. Barry found a place to disconnect the motor for a temporary solution. The dog would not get off my lap the whole night.

We took many trips with the Ellises in our motor homes. We were meeting at our favorite RV park in Red River, New Mexico. We checked in at the office to learn that we were one day early. They told us to go to the overload parking for 24 hours. Low and behold, the Ellises were parked there. They came a day early also. We had each made our reservations but had both made the same mistake.

Our favorite place was Red River, New Mexico. We camped there many times. The different adult kids and grandkids met us there over the years. We loved the Sunday church in the log community building downtown. On Sunday night, they would sing all the old hymns for an hour. It was such a blessing to take our grandchildren to the hymn singing over the years.

On one return trip home from Red River, we had a large inside tire on the motor home blow out while we were going about 65 miles per hour. As Barry said, God watches out for him on the road. Just down the road in deserted West Texas was a house with a few RV sites. We pulled in and learned the homeowner's best friend ran a truck with everything to change big truck tires just like our motor home tires. The homeowner called his friend, and we were back on the road.

Tammy and Grant were on this trip with us. Jeff was in med school. When the tire blew out, the steel peeled off and came through the bottom of the motor home. The motor home jumped up and down. The steel wore a hole through the bottom and the bottom of the closet slide-out. That was enough excitement for one day. When we got home, we found the ceiling along with the attic insulation in one bedroom was all over the floor. Dirt daubers had stopped up the outside air conditioner drain. We were thankful for insurance!

Our motorhome - many miles - much fun.

WE SAW EUROPE

In the fourth grade, each person in my class was to choose countries in Europe to make a report and present to the class. We had no TV. We had never seen what the Olde World countries looked like. Sometimes at the movies there would be a newsreel showing the destruction of World War II in Europe. You only saw piles of rubble.

I chose Holland and Switzerland to report on. I remember reading about people living in the Alps. I was in awe about all these different places. I knew no one who had ever been to such places except in war. I remember thinking how I would love to see these countries. I never ever dreamed that it would be possible for me to go to any country in Europe.

We have been to most of the European countries. Each time I would think every day that I was there how I had been blessed. I love exploring all the historical areas. After the kids were grown, we did one trip a year until we couldn't do it anymore because of health. I am so thankful that we did all this while we were young enough.

We took some of these trips with Tammy and Jeff. One trip was to the Czech Republic with Tammy, Jeff and Grant. Grant was 18 months old. So much fun!

We went to several countries with our friends David and Rosemary Kinzer. In England we were going down a highway to the next town when we had a blowout. Barry pulled over and there to all our amazement was an emergency phone. It is great to travel with Barry. Help is always there. He says God looks out for him. Barry called the rental car emergency number. They told him that someone would be there in 30 minutes. We put our suitcases to the side of the highway so the repairman could access the spare tire.

After some time, Rosemary and I were sitting on the suitcases and I said that it seemed like it had been 30 minutes. Rosemary in her calm slow Tennessee accent said, "I've been thinking about that. And, Prue, I have decided that when you are in a foreign country sitting on your suitcase on the side of the road, time just goes very, very slowly." She was right!

A repairman finally showed up and installed a new tire. Everything got put back together and we were on our way. That night we were headed to our bed and breakfast and it was getting dark. The lights shined straight down to the road. We could not see over three feet of road. We went oh so slowly. We told the bed and breakfast owners about this problem. The man showed Barry an adjustment on pointing the lights. Turns out, all English cars have this adjustment because of the fog. You learn a lot visiting other countries. We went on to enjoy the Cotswold Villages.

We saw Howard Castle. I was a Howard. We ate in the basement part of the castle. The food was some of the best we had in England. I told my dad's sister, Aunt Laura, about the food at the castle. She said, "Well, Prue, you know all of us Howards have always been good cooks." We both laughed.

We feel very blessed to be able to have seen so much in our lifetime. Most of it Barry did not even know that he wanted to see until I told him. He agrees that we really did need to see the world. We as other older husbands and wives sit and talk about all those precious memories.

KOCKLER CRITTERS, BIG AND SMALL

After a short time of marriage, Barry and I decided we really needed a puppy. We both had dogs most of our lives. We got a dog free which was half spitz and half rat terrier. We named him "Ralf." He weighed about 15 pounds at adulthood, was long-haired and was black and white like a rat terrier. Barry played with Ralf a lot while I was at work and he was between classes. Ralf was more the size of a rat terrier but thought he was a spitz. Spitz are known to like to fight, and he always joined in on a dog fight no matter how big the other dogs were.

Ralf had a lot of adjustments in his life as the children came along. Curtis was born and had colic. He cried a lot no matter what we did. Ralf would run into the bathroom under the footed bathtub. He would stay there until the crying stopped.

We moved to Kentucky. Curtis learned to crawl. Barry put knots in one of his ties. He never liked ties. Barry showed Curtis how to pull on the tie as he crawled. Ralf would pull on the other end while making playful growling noises. Curtis would get to laughing so hard he would fall on his stomach. They were the best of playmates.

Maybe this started Curtis' love of dogs. It was so cute to watch. What a joyful memory.

In North Carolina we stopped along the side of the road to look at a pop-up camper. All three boys got back in the car to go home. Curtis looked out the back of the car window and said, "Ralf is running behind us on the street." We pulled over and opened the door and he jumped in. He had been left behind.

In North Carolina a very large chow dog was chained in the yard behind us. It was barking. Ralf went over to bark at the chow. Ralf misjudged the length of the chain. Ralf ended up with a broken leg and some stitches. He had a cast on for a long time.

In the process of moving from North Carolina to Greeley, Colorado we camped for a couple of days with my mother and her husband Roy near Red River, New Mexico. They had stayed a week in a cabin there. Mother and Roy drove on towards Greeley following us in their car. In Walsenburg we stopped for gas. I changed Steve's diaper and took the other two boys to the bathroom.

We headed towards Colorado Springs where we had planned to spend the night. Going down the road, I saw a very large dog sitting in a very small sports car with its head sticking out the top. I said, "Look at that big dog." Just as I said this, I noticed that Ralf was not under my feet where he rode on trips. We could not get off the freeway until Colorado Springs because there were no outlets off the freeway until then. We got a motel. Barry called back to the gas station and asked them to hold the dog if they saw the dog. There were no cell phones then.

Barry and Roy drove back to Walsenburg to the gas station. There was no dog to be seen. Barry started to whistle over and over. Just as he was about to give up, he saw cornstalks in a very large cornfield starting to move. The movement kept coming toward him.

Finally, a very hot, tired and thirsty Ralf came to Barry. Poor Ralf just had to learn to take care of himself.

Later when we were in California, a boy came with his dog to play in our yard with Curtis and Keith. Ralf decided to chase the German Shepherd out of our yard. The large German Shepherd was not in the least scared of this little 15-pound dog. Ralf got stitches all the way around his midsection. That German Shepherd just about skinned him alive.

Our house in California was on a steep bank. To keep the dirt in place, ice plant was planted solid on the bank. Gophers love ice plant. They lived in their tunnels under the ice plant. Their favorite food was ice plant roots. If they kill all the ice plants the house might come down the bank in a heavy rain. Ralf could hear these gophers under the ground and would spend hours in hopes that one would stick its head up out of the ice plants. We put gopher traps in some of the holes. Ralf got his nose cut one time by a gopher trap from trying to get to the gophers. After that we quit using traps and put highway flares in the tunnels and tried to stop up the holes. The gas from the highway flares would kill the gophers. At least this is what we were told.

Ralf moved back to Texas with us. Later we were in our pop-up camper in the Smokies on a trip. Ralf went to the restroom with Barry and the boys and waited outside. It was getting dark. When Barry got back to the camper, he noticed Ralf was not with him. He went back to the restroom and found Ralf leaning against the building. Ralf could not see in the dark. He was getting old.

Ralf lived 16 years, through all the moves and the births and babyhoods of all the boys. He was always gentle with the boys no matter what. He died at home of natural causes. He had been a big part of our lives. We loved him!

We got a cockatiel bird. Somehow, I was convinced that with three boys to take care of I need a bird to sweep up after several times a day. Birds are messy!

Curtis, our big animal lover, would walk around with Pretty Boy on his shoulder. One day I was delivering some custom draperies. I got home and everyone was crying. Curtis had walked outside to feed Ralf forgetting Pretty Boy was on his shoulder. Just trying to ease the pain, I suggested we put the cage and stand on the front sidewalk. We put bird seed in it. Maybe Pretty Boy would get hungry and get back in the cage. One needs a wild imagination to raise a bunch of boys.

One week later a lady down the street called telling me there was an ad in the local paper about a cockatiel. I called the number and then went to her house. Her house was five miles away. She had long blond hair as I did at that time. She was in her back yard when our Pretty Boy landed on her shoulder. She walked into her house with Pretty Boy on her shoulder. She had a cage to put him in and got some bird seed. It turned out that I had done some draperies for the lady who had Pretty Boy. I paid her for the ad in the paper and for the bird feed. Oh, happy day!!!

After Ralf died, we got another dog. We named him Benny. He was half Pekingese and half Yorkshire Terrier. He was a loyal and loving dog. Benny always came and posed for every picture taken around here. No one called him. He just always came and sat down in the middle of the group. Benny had a more relaxing life than Ralf did. He was a good friend to all of us. He lived about 12 years.

After Bennie we had a series of Yorkshire Terriers. They do not live as long as mixed breeds. We now have a Maltese and Yorkshire Terrier mix. She is one of the smartest dogs we have had. She seems to know what I want her to do before I know and understands most everything we say.

In California, the boys had pet chameleons which change colors. I had to go buy live grasshoppers every week to feed them. One time the grasshoppers got loose in my car. That was fun!

The boys also had guinea pigs in California. We had a male and a female. You can go into guinea pig businesses real fast. They have babies really often. We gave the babies to the pet store to sell.

UNWANTED CRITTERS, BIG AND SMALL

We moved to the wilderness when we moved back to Texas. Our house was seven miles from town. Between town and us was nothing but farm and ranch land. We have been trying to tame this land for 48 years now.

The copperheads have slowed down now. We killed one or two a week at first. A couple of times they got in our house.

The first year we were here a possum decided to live on top of the riding lawnmower in the storage shed. It would poop on top of the motor. Every time Barry started the mower, possum poop would be slung from wall to wall of the shed and on Barry. The rest of us laughed but Barry did not think this funny. We ended up putting mothballs on top of the mower and around the outside of the shed. The possum found another home.

Squirrels have always and still are a headache. They love to chew holes in the wood to get in the attic. They plant pecan trees all over the yard. Most of these trees are not in good spots. We do have a couple of nice, large, pecan trees in good spots. The squirrels did that for us. Barry has trapped them for many years now to keep them thinned down. Barry also gets rats, possums and sometimes skunks in his trap. This is a good part-time job for Barry's semi-retirement.

One morning I came into the TV room. I had put Sally Mae, our Yorkshire Terrier, out in the fenced area earlier. She was barking very loudly. I looked out the window to see a skunk on top of Sally Mae with the skunk's teeth embedded into Sally Mae's head. I screamed for Barry to come. I told him the problem.

He said he was naked and was not going to fight a skunk when he did not have clothes on. I knew the skunk had rabies because they only bite when they have rabies. They also do not come out in the daylight unless they have rabies. I gave up on Barry and I saw a big beach towel on the ground. I went outside and grabbed the big beach towel. I threw the big towel around the skunk. A skunk will not spray if they cannot get their tail up. With the towel all around the skunk, I put my hands around the back of the skunk's neck and pulled the skunk off the little dog. The skunk would not let go of the dog at first. When I picked the skunk up, the dog came up also. I shook the skunk, and the dog came loose. I wrapped the towel tight as I could around the skunk. I had hoped that the skunk would stay in the towel until Barry got there with his gun. Sally Mae ran through the door to the inside of the house. She ran barking through the whole house. The skunk smell was all over Sally Mae. Therefore, the whole house smelled like skunk. I shut the door and ran into the house. The skunk got loose from the towel and stood on its back legs looking through the window in the door. She was still looking for that little dog.

Barry took Sally Mae to the vet. She was fine and was good with her rabies shot. The house smelled bad, as did the dog, for a long time. And, yes, I tried every trick in the book to get rid of the smell. I was told by the vet that once a skunk bites or comes out in daylight, it is only two to three days from dying. My house and dog still smelled like skunk long after that skunk went to skunk heaven.

CHAPTER 11

Our Precious Grandchildren

We became grandparents in our early 40s. Alisha was our first grandchild. Tammy was only eight years old when she became an aunt. Tammy was closer in age to Alisha than to any of her brothers. They were more like sisters. Tammy was always there to take care of Alisha. The first child and the first grandchild are always special in the heart. Alisha was always one step ahead of you with her mouth.

One day, her mother and I took her to a fabric store. She kept pulling bolts of fabric down on the floor. Finally, her mother smacked her hands! As we got in the car, her mother was just about to start in on her. Before her mother could say a word, Alisha said, "Mom, I was very disappointed in the way you acted in that store. You hit my hands two times." I was trying not to laugh. Alisha was two years old then. The mouth was what got her in trouble, but oh, how we loved and still love that girl. She has a fine husband, Chas. We are so glad to have him in our family now. They have Aspyn our first great grandchild. Oh, she is so special to us.

Alisha and our wonderful great granddaughter Aspyn.

Alisha's brother Tyler came a couple of years after she was born. He was always a fun-loving child, but the most stubborn child I have dealt with. I kept Alisha and Tyler a lot for their mother to work part-time in Barry's consulting business. She is an accountant. One day I was putting Tyler in the corner. When all else failed, he would have to sit in the corner. On the way to the corner he said, "When I grow up, I am going to build a round house without a corner to sit in." Tyler was two years old at that time. He was and is a joy to us always.

Tyler was about nine years old when Steve's son Hunter was born. Hunter was always full of confidence and was always coming up with something to do that you never thought about him doing. I kept him and later his brother Gabriel two days a week while their mother taught school.

One day Hunter had a little fishing pole with a toy fish with magnets on them. He put the fish in the dog cage. He fished down from the top cage with the pole which had a magnet on it. As he reeled the fish in through the wire mesh on top of the cage, the fish caught on the wire. He pulled harder and harder until the fish popped out and up into the pupil of his eye. It cut his eyeball. I was just in the next room. Hunter was crying but screamed out, "I caught a fish!" His eye did not have permanent damage. His mother came to take him to the doctor. He told everyone about catching a fish. Hunter now has a beautiful wife, Victoria. They were married in our back yard.

Hunter and Victoria Kockler's wedding in Barry and Prue's backyard.

Keith and Kelli's first daughter was Makayla. Her middle name is Joy, named for me. Makayla was and is a beautiful girl. One of the big blessings of Barry's and my lives has been having Makayla and her little sister Lani grow up three doors down from our house. Her dad is a policeman. Makayla's mother is an airline attendant. If Keith was called to go in to work in the middle of the night and Kelli was out of town, the girls would be brought down to our house to sleep. Makayla would be surprised to wake up at our house. She would sit up in bed and look around and say, "Someone must have been bad in Richardson last night."

Makayla loved playing with her cousins when they were all here at our house. She led everyone in what to play. They all loved her ideas, and all had so much fun. She is now in her third year of college.

Gabriel was born when Hunter was four years old. Gabriel always loved his big brother Hunter better than anyone. He was a calm loving child. I rocked him a lot. We both liked that a lot. Gabriel was a little clown. He was so happy and loved to make people laugh. He has brought us great joy. Gabriel loves music and computers and is a good artist.

Our Precious Grandchildren

Lani Grace was born about two years after her sister Makayla. She was happy most of the time, but if she got unhappy her eyes would let you know right away. Lani and Makayla stayed with me when both parents were working.

One day I put Lani down for a nap in a spare bedroom. She was in a porta crib. Just barely in her reach on the bed was a container of spools of thread. She got hold of the thread end of one spool and turned around and around until the spool was empty. She did this with many spools of thread. The thread was tight up and down her whole body. Finally, she could not move and started crying like she was really in pain. I came in and could not believe my eyes. I could not bend this child because the thread was so tight up and down her body. I held her down and started cutting the threads. She was scared and would not be still. I was afraid that I would cut her with the scissors. What would the world be without children to keep us humble. My beautiful Lani Grace left our street this week for college. This is hard for me. Lani likes to antique with me. God has blessed us so, so much!

Tammy and Jeff have Grant who is now 17 years old. He is a handsome, smart and wonderful guy! We had wonderful times in the motor home with all the grandkids. Grant loved the motor home more than anything when he was young. He was riding with Barry and me in the motor home coming home from a trip. Tammy and Jeff were following in their car. We had to stop in Sherman to move Grant to the car with his parents. Sherman is where they took a different road to go home. Grant was not going to let go of the motor home seat. It took all of us to get him out of the motor home! He was stubborn at that time. He knew what he wanted. I am sure that he still knows what he wants, but he is quieter about everything now. He spent a lot of time with us when Tammy was helping with

Barry's foundation reports. We have been able to have a lot of time with Grant and we are so thankful for it. Now he plays a lot of basketball.

Christmas 2018 at the Lilly house – Jeff, Tammy, Keith, Kelli, Steve, Stacey, Chas, Alisha, Aspyn, Tyler, Krystal.

Our sweet Charlotte Faith just turned 14 years old. She loves babies just as I always have. She took such good care of her two younger brothers. In fact, you could say she spoiled Creed. Charlotte has such a sweet and loving heart. She loves to cook and sew just as I did, growing up. A couple of years ago, Charlotte and I made sweet pickles and canned them together. Charlotte loves school and joins everything. She is in choir, volleyball, theatre, and basketball. She does well at all of them. She has a beautiful voice.

Clark Howard Lilly and Hannah Belle Kockler are four months apart. Hannah is older. She is Steve and Stacey's daughter. She is a very social girl. She has lots of friends. She loves everyone. She is beautiful and loves theatre arts. She also loves school and does very well. She has a beautiful singing voice. We always love the time we have with her. We enjoy her bringing her friends to swim in our pool.

Clark is very smart. He is Jeff and Tammy's second son. He is a real boy and sometimes enjoys his friends at school more than the studying, but he does well in school. He reads all the time. For his birthdays we usually go to the bookstore to shop. He is always interested in my ancestry work and likes to hear about different ones in our ancestry. Clark just turned 10 years old as did Hannah. They are in two different grades because of the months they were born. They play together a lot and are good to include Creed also.

Creed is the baby of the grandchildren. He is Tammy and Jeff's third son. He is full of fun. He started kindergarten this week. He loves learning and is already reading. He is large for his age. He will be our gentle giant. Creed thinks that Charlotte can do everything he wants her to do. She usually gives it her best to please him. Creed is a very good swimmer. He may turn out to be a very good athlete. I do know for sure that he is a treasure to us.

Emily is our grandchild who came into our family when her mother married our son Curtis. Emily was in middle school when Curtis and Victoria married and in the same grade as Alisha. She fit right into our family. After college, she went into the Navy. Barry and I were privileged to attend her induction ceremony into the Navy. We were so proud. She married a fine Air Force man. They have two little boys and live in Colorado Springs now.

I want to include Annie. She was the precious child of Barry's cousin (stepsister) in Pennsylvania. She grew up to be a lovely woman. She went in the military from high school. She went through college and she stayed in the military for a long time. She married a fine man who is a lawyer in the military (Jags). They have two beautiful young girls and have just been transferred to Germany. I am so proud of Annie.

We have a great granddaughter, Aspyn. For now, she lives in Germany with her mother and dad. We miss her so much. This is Alisha's and Chas's adorable little red-headed girl. She will soon be two years old. We talk to her on Facetime. The China virus has kept them from coming back for a visit. We look forward to holding her soon. I still have a closet full of toys for her to play with. I have never had a time that I did not have toys in the house for a little one. That is just the way I wanted it to be. I cannot imagine life without little ones. The more, the merrier.

Lani, Makayla, Charlotte, Grant, Hunter, and Gabriel having fun.

Grandchildren in the Magnolia tree as usual.

Christmas with grandkids.

CHAPTER 12

My Parents

After my parents' divorce, my mother moved to Oklahoma City and worked in the trust department at a bank. After a couple of years, she met Roy Black. They married and had a wonderful 25 years of marriage.

Mother came to Kentucky and I made the dress she wore for their wedding. I flew down to be with her for the wedding. We all loved Roy dearly. Everyone loved Roy.

Roy was the son of a Methodist minister. He had gone in the Navy out of high school. World War II came along. His ship was torpedoed. There was water in the bottom section with men's bodies in the water. Men were diving into the water to get the men's bodies out.

One of the divers got sick the next day so Roy took that man's diver's helmet and finished getting the last bodies out. It turned out that the diver who used the helmet first had Tuberculosis. Roy came down with Tuberculosis soon. It was at the end of the war. Roy was in government hospitals for some years. By the time it was all over, Roy only had part of one lung. He did live but lived the rest of his life without much energy. He went to OSU at Oklahoma City and got his degree. He worked until retirement at the OSU campus in Oklahoma City. My mother kept him moving and traveling which was probably good for him.

My mother sold real estate and did well at it. She always was self-driven in whatever she did. She made enough money for them to build a very nice home in a very nice part of Oklahoma City.

Roy lived longer than any of the doctors thought he would with the lung problems. It was hard on his heart. My mother did not do well accepting his death. She lived about 10 years after Roy died. She died at 84 years old. She did remarry, but that was not good.

My dad did not go back to the farm as I thought he would. He always said he wanted to go back to the farm. A couple of years after the divorce he married Gionith. She was perfect for him. She took care of him like his mother, then his sister, then my mother and later like I did. Gionith was a friend of Aunt Lorah (Dad's sister).

Gionith didn't have big desires for much in material things. She had been married but had no children. She took our kids as her grandchildren. She was a good grandmother.

My dad always played 42 at work. Gionith had grown up playing 42. Barry and I played 42 with them often. Curtis and Keith would go to stay several days with them in the summer in Fort Worth. Dad had the boys playing 42 before long.

Dad was several years older than Gionith. My dad was always heavy, sometimes 275 pounds. He did not exercise and ate the wrong things. Gionith walked the track every day and ate what she should. I never dreamed that my dad would outlive Gionith, but he did. She had a heart attack in her mid '60s. I thought I would end up taking care of Gionith in her old age. She would have been easy to take care of. I will talk later about taking care of my dad until his death at age 89.

My mother and me in Florida revisiting War memories.

Keith, Steve, Grandma Maude, Curtis, Tammy, and Alisha at Steve's high school graduation.

Spending Sprees-Sweepstakes

Before Gionith died she took me to the bank and had me sign for access to her safe deposit box. I did not dream that anything was wrong with her or I would have asked more questions and would have tried to handle everything better. When she died, my dad went to the safe deposit box and got lots of savings bonds out. He had no idea that she had saved that money. If he had, he would have made her let him spend the money.

He bought a new car. I told him to be sure and get the insurance on the new car. He said not to worry, that he was sure the car dealership had taken care of that. Gionith did all the driving. I knew he was now a terrible driver. Within a week, he ran into a carload of people. The other car was totaled, and his new car had $10,000 of damage. Thankfully, the time was within the grace period of getting the insurance changed. There were lots of injured people in the other car.

Soon one of his two bedrooms was stacked to the ceiling solid with junk he had bought to increase his chance of winning a sweepstakes. He went down to the bank where Gionith had worked and cashed her whole IRA out. He spent it all. Whenever you talked to my dad, he always told you that he had 1.3 million or 2.4 million or maybe 5 million coming in next week when he won the sweepstakes. He got so much sweepstakes mail that it was delivered each day in a large mail container.

I talked to his doctor and he said I should go to court and have my dad declared mentally incompetent. I would have to sit in front of him in court to do this. I was all that my dad had. He would have never spoken to me again if I had done this. I could not do it. Barry and I decided to wait until all his money was gone. He did get Social Security and a small retirement check from Bell. We would just have to make up the difference from that to what he needed.

My dad ate breakfast at the same place each morning. I am sure the help there had heard about the 1.2 million or whatever he was about to get. One of the women had no place to live. She was in her mid-30s and was a meth addict and a drunk. She moved in with my dad. She had a boyfriend who came often. When dad's check came in, he would give it and the car keys to her to go buy groceries. Three or four days later, he would call me hungry and to tell me that the police had impounded his car. Over to Fort Worth we would go and pay to get the car from the police impoundment. The car would have been lived in by bums and such. We would go with him to buy groceries. We did not want him to drive. In a day or two, dad would get a call from the woman to come to bail her out of jail. This happened many times. The Bible says that I am to honor my father. I cannot let him go hungry.

The IRS called me because my dad did not pay income tax from Gionith's IRA. The bank where Gionith had worked loaned him $10,000 with no collateral. The bank called me about this loan. They said my dad had told them that he was going to get 1 something million next week. They said that they thought he might have some mental problems. I told them that their loan officer who loaned money to an old man who had no income and no collateral must have some mental problems also. Both the bank and the IRS thought we should pay this for my dad. Barry and I went to a lawyer and had him mail a letter telling the bank and the IRS that we did not owe them anything. The lawyer told them to call him, not us. Of course, they gave up.

I had suggested to dad that we should get down to the courthouse and do a quick deed to transfer the house to me. I would then have that money to take care of him. He agreed and we did it. The next week the woman and her boyfriend returned and wanted to take dad down to get a loan on his house because he was out of money. They had been taking his money every chance they could to support their drug habits. Dad told me that the woman and her boyfriend had explained to him that I had stolen his house from him. He was mad.

Finally, the meth addict went to prison. Dad went into assisted living. I had the money to pay for his assisted living for a while. We did run out. The house only sold for $25,000. When that was gone, we paid it with our money. I was just so thankful that the woman and her boyfriend had not killed him. I prayed a lot about all this for those years.

All the family came over to help clean out Dad's house. The sweepstakes papers were in everything. The freezer was full. The oven was full. Boxes were stacked to the ceiling full of sweepstakes papers. You had to look at every paper because right in the middle would be the car title or some other important paper.

Later as he Dad became less able to care for himself I wanted Dad to move to a nursing home close to me. He would not leave the assisted living center because he wanted to stay in Fort Worth. He said he knew his way around in Fort Worth (even though he never left the building). He needed more care than he had been getting. In the assisted living he fell and broke his ankle. He would not let anyone take him to the hospital. We went to Fort Worth. I told him he had to go to the hospital. He said that he was fine. He had been on the floor for almost 15 hours, I think. He said he was fine on the floor. I said what about going to the bathroom. He explained that he was just fine on the floor. He just peed into a pillow. I explained to him that this was not an acceptable lifestyle. Finally, he agreed to go to the hospital.

From the hospital, we moved Dad to a nursing home in Flower Mound. Things were better. The nursing home workers loved my dad because he joked with them a lot. He did not complain. If you asked him what he needed he would tell you that he had everything a man could want. My thought was, "So why did you try so hard for money from sweepstakes?"

One day the nursing home called me to tell me my dad was crying, and they did not know why. I went there and he told me that he had learned the physical therapy lady was married and had two small kids. She had told him that she was going to marry him. He believed that this young lady was going to marry him. He always thought every lady around was in love with him. He still thought this was true. He had spent his bingo chips that he had won on a gown for this physical therapy nurse. I guess that was when she decided to tell him that she was married. She never dreamed that he believed she was going to marry him. She did not really know him.

Dad had a feeding tube in the hospital but was later able to have it taken out. He enjoyed eating always. Through physical therapy on his throat, he was able to swallow his food again. He spent his last couple years at the nursing home in Flower Mound enjoying going to the dining room to eat. The throat problem did come back over a year later. It allowed his food to go into his lungs. The therapist tried again but could not help this time. There was no long illness nor pain. He just slept away.

I could write a book full of all that went on with my dad after Gionith died. As Barry said in the middle of it all, no matter what was going on, Dad was always good for a laugh. I was so thankful for Barry's patience with my dad during those years. I could not have made it through it all without Barry. Of course, that is the way of my life. God gave me Barry to help me get through the difficult times and to celebrate the good times. We have had a lot of good times to celebrate. We have been blessed.

JANE LOUISE

Speaking of older relatives, I would take my mother-in-law whenever she was in town to see her cousin in Arlington. This was Jane Louise who had a grown son living with her. Not only did I never see this son, Tim, but my mother-in-law never saw him during her visits over a 20-year time period. My mother-in-law, Maude, started teasing that she sometimes wondered if Tim really existed.

Years earlier, Tim came home from college and became a hermit in his bedroom. He said he was in pain all the time and he said that he could not see well enough to get around. The doctors (there were many) said that his pain was all mental and that he could see perfectly if he only wore his glasses.

Tim had long ago had a motorcycle accident and that caused damage to his nose, according to him. This is why he would not wear his glasses. He said that the glasses hurt his nose. One thing that everyone agreed on about Tim was that he took a lot of all kinds of drugs including hallucinogens while in college. This was Jane's only child and she and her husband had spent everything they had on trying to help Tim get well. By the time I spent much time with Jane, her husband had died, and all the money was gone.

Jane Louise was fighting lung cancer by the time I was called by a social worker to help Jane Louise take care of her finances. I would write her bills from her Social Security check and take money from her little check to give to Tim for his groceries. Jane Louise was in the hospital unable to do anything. Tim never left his apartment. Jane Louise's Episcopal priest would pick up Tim's groceries.

I was told to find Jane Louise a nursing home. She told me she would prefer to stay in a nursing home close to me. She was afraid of Tim with good reason.

I went to see Jane Louise at the nursing home every day unless I was out of town. If I were out of town, I asked someone to check on her and report to me each day. Every few weeks Barry and I would go to Arlington to get Tim and bring him to see his mother while we were there with them. Then we would take him home. This was an hour each way, which meant four hours before we got home. Every time we tried to arrange this visit for Tim, he would be very difficult to agree on a day for this. I never went around Tim without Barry with me. Tim was a big man and an angry man. He did want to see his mother. In the car, we had to pull over and stop the car every ten minutes or so. This was because he had to put liquid in one eye every ten minutes. He told us every time that he had to put water in his eye often or he would lose what little eyesight he had left. These days were difficult long days when we took Tim to see his mother.

After about a year in the nursing home, Jane Louise died in her sleep. Other than Tim, we were all the family in Texas that Jane Louise had. We talked to the social worker about Tim. He could not stay in the apartment because the Social Security check was no longer there to pay the rent. The social worker had two people to come to see Tim about a home that he could go in with other people like himself. He said he would think about it and in the meantime, he had the priest sell the nice piano and a few other things that had a little value. That paid for his food and rent for a few months.

I had heard that Tim grew marijuana plants in his closet. He did not get out to sell any, but he was a heavy user. I thought that he probably would not leave his plants to move anyplace. Jane Louise and Tim had lived there for about 25 years.

Then one day the apartment manager called me to say that Tim had killed himself in the apartment. Before I could leave to go to Arlington, the police called me. They were at the apartment. They asked me if I knew anything about the foil wrapped closet with growing lights. I told the policeman that my son was a policeman and that our family had nothing to do with any of that. I asked the police to please take the plants with them.

There was no money to pay for a funeral other than our money. Tim's parents were both cremated and they had a place for their ashes to be put at Bishop Mason's Retreat in Flower Mound.

Jane Louise's priest said they had a place under their alter at his church to put ashes and they would donate a place for Tim's ashes. We paid for the cremation and funeral services. Tim was an atheist. I got a little smile from my darker side about Tim's ashes being under the altar.

Our whole family went to Tim's apartment with us to clear it out. My plan was to sell as much as I could to pay the funeral expenses that we had paid.

We brought all we thought we might be able to sell to our house for a garage sale. There was a beautiful solid cherry bedroom set. It was so heavy. We rented a trailer to put it all in. The bedroom set had been Jane Louise's father's set. Her father had a lot of money. He was a steel advisor of President Truman. Her father was from Pennsylvania and had been in the steel industry all his life.

I found a tea set in the top of the kitchen cabinet. It was covered with decades of cigarette smoke and was just dark gray. I put them in a basket to bring home to wash up. This tea set had flowers all over it. This set was the beginning of my antique chintz dish collection. Even though I was in the antique business at the time, I did not know about chintz dishes. They started coming on the antique market shortly after this time. They became very expensive. I just knew that I liked them. Now the chintz has gone down in price but I still like them.

Tim had quit taking out garbage and quit throwing anything away. What a mess! At the very end he threw his silverware and dishes in the garbage as he used it. He knew what he was going to do.

We were about ready to leave when I saw an antique chest of drawers and a table covered by Tim's bed. The apartment people told us to leave what we did not want. They were going to gut the apartment and redo it. Barry told me to leave all that because there was blood and brains on the table. That was where Tim had shot himself. I told Barry there was no kind of matter that could stand between me and an antique.

The table held boxes of files of the different kinds of plants that were in Tim's closet. It held records of years and years of details about measurements of water and fertilizer in each plant.

Under all his plant records and all kinds of matter was a beautiful oval marble topped Victorian table. It matched two small Victorian chairs. I would later learn from my mother-in-law that those two chairs and the marble topped table had set in the entry hall of hers and Jane Louise's grandmother's home. They had belonged to Barry's great grandmother.

Do you remember my telling you earlier about my grandmother throwing her bread upon the water when helping her neighbor on Christmas Day? I threw my bread upon the water. This is one of those miracles. I did what I could for Jane Louise with no thoughts of ever getting anything in return. We paid for the funeral and had a garage sale. We sold enough to pay for the funeral with $5 over. Besides, I was able to have three homemade quilts which were made by Barry's great grandmother. That would be my grandchildren's great, great, great grandmother. I also got the beautiful floral chintz dishes and the Victorian chairs and table. I threw my bread upon the water. Look what God brought back to me. Our God is a

God of miracles. As you go through the journey of your life, keep your eyes open for the miracles God will perform for you. Look for God's fingerprints.

Throw your bread upon the water. After many days it may return to you.

Remember our God is a God of Miracles.

CHAPTER 13

Wisdom Learned Along the Way

Grandchildren, when you start to date, please only date someone who would be a good mate. You will fall in love with a person with whom you date. Be sure that you date people who would be a good match for you and that they have the same values you have. Don't believe in love at first sight. That is not called love. How can you love someone before you know their heart? You may think that you will worry about those things when you are older. Many people start dating their young love and never stopped dating that person. Tammy and Jeff started dating in high school. Barry and I started dating young.

I had not planned to marry Barry when I first started dating him. Some of the happiest marriages I have known started dating young. They dated for a long time before marriage. They had lots of time to know if they wanted the same things in life.

Sometimes I hear of a couple who have married and then discuss if they want children. Learn these things about each other while you are dating. Do you both want to gain great wealth more than other things in life? What is important to you both? It is better to learn these things before you get married than to try to change each other after you get married.

Please think along the early part of your life journey what things are important to you. If you want to live a Christian life, pray about these things.

I know you are all going to make, with God's help, a wonderful life for yourself. Please remember life is a journey, not a destination.

Kockler/Lilly Vacation in Telluride, Colorado. Barry, Prue, Keith/Kelli – Makayla and Lani, Steve/Stacey – Gabriel and Hannah, Jeff/Tammy Lilly – Grant, Charlotte, Clark, and Creed.

WHAT DID I WANT? WHAT DO I WANT?

Barry and I made the decision to marry before he was out of college. We knew that this decision would mean that I would be a longer period before we could buy a house and live a more comfortable life. We were willing to accept this reality. We both knew we wanted a large family.

Growing up, I dreamed about living in a yellow house with a large front porch with white wicker furniture. I wanted a gazebo in the back yard and a Weeping Willow in the front yard. I planted a Weeping Willow tree in our back yard when I was 15 years old.

My dad thought that girls should always stay home. If I went to a sleepover with a girlfriend or most any other thing, he would get mad at me. He would trim the Weeping Willow tree. When I got married years later, my tree was about 18 feet tall but with not a branch on it. It was a straight stick with one branch on top Weeping to one side only.

Barry says that he has paid over and over for my dad's trimming of my Weeping Willow at home. Barry also says that he could have retired years ago but for all the Weeping Willow trees he has had to buy. Texas is not the easiest place to grow Weeping Willow trees. They like lots of water.

One by one, Barry and I, with God's help, achieved our dreams. We raised the roof and moved it forward to make a large front porch some years ago. When no one else was painting brick houses, we painted our bricks yellow.

Home in Double Oak, Texas.

Our home is certainly not the biggest nor the fanciest home around, but it is exactly just what we want. It is home. We have lived here 48 years. We praise God for all we have. There is a song that I love that says:

> *Thank You, Lord, For Your Blessings On Me*
> *There's a roof up above me*
> *I've a good place to sleep*
> *There's food on my table*
> *And shoes on my feet*
> *You gave me your love, Lord*
> *And a fine family*
> *Thank you, Lord, for your blessings on me.*

There were times in my life when I was young that the list above was all that I did have. I was happy and thankful then. But now look at all the blessings the Lord has bestowed on me. Sometimes I close my eyes and can hardly believe it.

FROM ICY ROADS TO EASTER EGG HUNTS

There was a cold winter morning with thick ice on all the roads. Barry and I were slowly traveling on the worst ice storm roads of my many years. We were the only car on many of the roads that day other than cars off in ditches. We were on our way to Jeff's and Tammy's house. Our grandson Grant had a round growth on the back of his head. The growth was growing rapidly. His appointment for his MRI was that day. We had to get there. Jeff was working at the hospital. Doctors cannot take time off for such things.

Thankfully, we had a four-wheel drive vehicle. At last, we made it to the house. Barry, Tammy and Grant were on their way to the hospital in our car. I stayed with the other children. Soon Grant was tested and scheduled for surgery. He had a Langerhans cell histiocytosis. Everything went well. Prayers were answered. It is scary for a doctor to cut a hole in a seven-year-old boy's skull.

We had planned to go to South Padre Island to meet our friends the Ellises for two weeks in the motor home. We postponed that trip until after Grant's surgery. When we came home from South Padre Island, spring had arrived in our back yard. I walked out to the gazebo to enjoy what now was a beautiful back yard. The leaves had come out in that beautiful color of new spring green. The grass was green. I was praising God. The icy road and winter and Grant's surgery were all in the past. I should do something to celebrate and to praise God!! My mind was flooded with "Easter Egg Hunt."

Our yard was perfect for an Easter egg hunt. This was the start of years of Easter egg hunts. All year I would watch as new people moved into Double Oak. If there were signs of young children in the yard, I would come to their door that week before Easter and invite them to egg hunt. The parents came also.

While older children hid the eggs in the back yard, I would read a book about the first Easter to the younger children on the front porch. After the hunt, we all ate lunch from the gazebo.

People may not be open to accepting an invitation to church from someone who knocks on their door. They will likely accept an invitation to bring their children to an Easter egg hunt. After the hunt, we always invited everyone to Easter church.

I invited the grandchildren of my friends also. We were able to watch our friends' grandchildren grow up. Some of my children's friends growing up also came with their children. We usually had 50 or 60 people attend. It was a wonderful day.

We would fill hundreds of eggs with candy, coins and little papers of scripture. We moved all the outdoor yard furniture around the gazebo. All this, and the food was a lot of work, but we loved doing it. But the time came when we were no longer physically able to do it.

Ecclesiastes 3:1, *For everything there is a season, and a time for every purpose under heaven; a time to be born and a time to die..."* and a time for an Easter egg hunt.

We do miss it! We are so thankful for the seasons we were able to have our Easter egg hunt and tell all the new Double Oak children about the first Easter.

Learning about Jesus on our front porch during Easter egg hunt.

RockPointe

The church we were in before we found RockPointe had been a great church. All of a sudden, something seemed very different with the minister's teaching. For several months the sermon was the same, week after week. We were taught that we were never to ask for forgiveness from God. We had grace and that was it. Finally, we started to look at other churches. We could not seem to find one we felt was the one for us.

I had prayed for God to lead us to the right church for us to worship and serve. In the middle of this search, our Supper Club group went to Atlanta to visit the Supper Club couple who had moved away from this area years earlier.

We had a wonderful visit and were at the Atlanta airport awaiting our flight home. A young woman started yelling and running toward our group. Three of the ladies in our group became very excited to see this young lady. Turns out, she had grown up in the church of these three ladies in our Supper Club. She told me that all three of my friends had taught her in Sunday School as she grew up. Her name was Jennifer.

Jennifer told us all that she had visited Andy Stanley's church to learn about their children's education program. She continued on that she was working at a start-up church. She had the job of starting their elementary education program. I asked the name of her church. She said that it was meeting in a school in Highland Village and its name was RockPointe.

I had prayed to God to help us to find the church where we needed to be. I never dreamed this help would come in the Atlanta airport. God works in mysterious ways. We visited RockPointe the next Sunday. We knew that RockPointe Church was where God led us through Jennifer in the Atlanta airport.

Soon, one by one, three of our kids and their families came to RockPointe. Tammy, Jeff and family were living in Carrollton at the time we started to attend RockPointe. Now they live in Flower Mound and go to RockPointe. We usually sit together and go out to eat together each Sunday. I sit in our long row each Sunday and thank God. Not many people have a lot of family who are able to worship together in this day and time. The cousins love being in church together. Most of them have been on mission trips together. We have all been so very blessed to be a part of the church of RockPointe.

Just two weeks after we left our old church for RockPointe, the minister of the old church had to leave because he was having an affair. It was so sad for the church. My mother died at this same time under difficult circumstances. God knew that I did not need to be in all the added stress going on in the old church. I needed spiritual nourishment, not turmoil when my mother died. I was where I needed to be. God made sure of that. Our God is a God of miracles. Look for those miracles as you go through your life's journey. Look for God's fingerprints.

GOOD TIMES – BAD TIMES

When my children were married, the wedding ceremonies were also adoption ceremonies for me. When the husbands and wives of my children joined our family, they became my children. I truly love them as my own children.

If these families break up, I suffered from the loss in my own heart and the sadness of my child and mostly the sadness of my grandchildren. I remember thinking when I bent over sometimes that my heart was going to fall out of my chest. The heart felt so heavy and I can remember thinking that I had to remind myself to breathe. If someone chooses to leave your family, you can do nothing but lean on God until time passes. The loss is always there, but you can learn to live your life again.

Family is so important to me. I want to protect my family always, but I cannot protect them always. My hope and prayer is that they will all learn to trust God. I hope and pray that they will all choose to follow Jesus. If we follow the teachings in the Bible, we will be protected from some of the pitfalls in life's journey. But we live in a fallen world, and we will all suffer through times of great pain. I will be praying for all of you every day that I live.

I got a Bible when I was 7 years old. My mother wrote in the front page, "May your every thought and every step you take in life be directed by the words in this book." I carried this Bible in my wedding with the flowers attached to it.

CHAPTER 14

Small Glimpses of Memorable Moments

I was born in the middle of WWII, not the best time to enter this world. No one knew if Hitler, in the end, would rule the world. Americans were full of trust and hope and continued with their lives and raised their families.

After the war, I lived on the farm and spend my evenings catching lightening bugs. I put them in a jar with small holes in the lid. They were the night light in my room.

Once, my mother and I rode a bus to Tulsa to visit my mother's sister and her family. We went to a high school auditorium and watch Bob Wills and his Texas Playboys sing and play their music known as Texas Swing. This group later became very famous and no longer played in high school auditoriums!

After moving to Ft. Worth, Aunt Lorah made me a dress. She was a wonderful seamstress. The fabric was a little stiff and itched my arms. I told Aunt Lorah about this problem. This is when I learned a great lesson. She told me, "sometimes it hurts to be pretty."

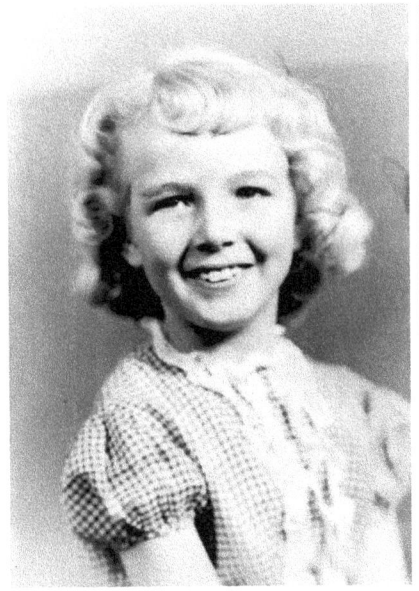

My pretty dress the itched. *Aunt Lorah at age 84.*

When I graduated from high school, I had a graduation tea with two of my friends. This was done by many graduating girls at that time in the south. Your friends would come dressed in their very best with gloves and high heeled shoes.

We had fancy foods and punch. We visited and talked a lot about our future plans. It was a special time with your friends who would all be going in different directions. As a grandmother I have had Blessing Tea's for all my granddaughter's when they turn 13. This is a time that ladies who know and love them come to celebrate and share Godly advice as they begin their journey to become Godly women. It's a special time of prayer and blessings.

High School Graduation Tea.

Blessing Tea for Lani Grace Kockler.

When we lived in North Carolina we were at a Sunday school party in a home of one of the members of the class. We watched the first man walk on the moon together on their TV. It was a special time. Americans all loved their country and were happy to show their love for their country. I am still so happy that I was born in the United States of America!

When we moved to our present home it was not within any city limits. The residents decided to incorporate into a town because we did not want to be taken in to Flower Mound. We felt we would have higher taxes for very little services.

There was an old country school just down the road from the old Bartonville store. The school had been closed for many years, and someone was living in the old school building. The name of the school was Hawks Double Oak. This is where we got the name of Double Oak for our new town. Some years later, the school building burned.

WHEN WILL I BE OLD?

I have asked myself this question the last few years. I was walking in the hall at church at Bible study the day after I had gotten my first hearing aids. I felt something on my shoulder. I felt with my hand and realized that my hearing aid was out and hanging on my earrings. I remember thinking, "This may be old age."

We had a long two years of orthopedic surgery. I had my neck fused in two places to help with pain in the arm. Barry had his back fixed with lots of metal and screws. The doctor came in from his front and from his back. Months later, Barry had his neck fused as I had. The same year, he had a shoulder replacement. The next year, he had a knee and then a hip replaced. We really felt old that year, but after recovering from all the surgeries, we felt younger. Barry has 33 screws and a lot of other metal in his body but fortunately his body accepts metal.

One thing is for sure, there are fewer years ahead than the years that I have behind me. So, Lord, what should I do in the years ahead that I have not done in the past? What can I do for my family? You have just read what I have worked on for the past year. One other thing I started doing a few years ago is to pick up one picture of a grandchild and hold it to my heart and pray for that grandchild. I pray for what I know or think that child is going through at that time.

At church, the minister asks people in the congregation to stand if they are in special need of prayer. Those in the congregation sitting near the one standing will put their hands on them as the minister leads congregational prayer. My holding my grandchild's picture to my heart is like putting my hands on them to me. I pray specifically for that grandchild. There are pictures everywhere of my grandchildren. This is something I can do even if I am old.

Goodbye Kisses

Barry and I make more of a point to kiss goodbye when one of us leaves the other to go do whatever. We are both old enough to think that if something should happen to one of us, we want the last kiss or "I love you" to be remembered.

I am so thankful for my life's journey. I have been so blessed. I know my final destination when this life is over, and I am very excited about that destination.

I pray that each and every one who reads this book has a wonderful journey and final destination. If you do not believe in the God of Miracles, please read *I Don't Have Enough Faith to Be an Atheist* by Norman L Geisler.

With all my love,
Prue, AKA Mema

Victory in Jesus
(Barry and my favorite hymn)

I heard an old, old story
How a Savior came from glory
How He gave His life on Calvary
To save a wretch like me
I heard about His groaning
Of His precious blood's atoning
Then I repented of my sins
And won the victory

O victory in Jesus
My Savior, forever
He sought me and bought me
With His redeeming blood
He loved me ere I knew Him
And all my love is due Him
He plunged me to victory
Beneath the cleansing flood

I heard about His healing
Of His cleansing pow'r revealing
How He made the lame to walk again
And caused the blind to see
And then I cried, "Dear Jesus
Come and heal my broken spirit"
And somehow Jesus came and brought
To me the victory

I heard about a mansion
He has built for me in glory
And I heard about the streets of gold
Beyond the crystal sea
About the angels singing
And the old redemption story
And some sweet day I'll sing up there
The song of victory

APPENDIX

Those Who Came Before

All who know me know that I love history and I love studying ancestry. Knowing those families' stories, their struggles and how and where they lived helps us appreciate the lives we live today.

PETER KOCKLER

I remember visiting St. Wendel, Germany, standing in the very old Catholic Church in the middle of the square. There were plaques on the wall listing young men from the town who lost their lives in World War I. There were several Kocklers listed.

As I stood there reading those names, I remembered visiting two of Barry's great uncles in Akron, Ohio. They were in World War I fighting against these German cousins. Barry's great grandfather came to the U.S. from the little town of St. Wendel, Germany that is now 20,000 in population. He was 18 years old when he came by himself. His family made barrels for the wine industry. He landed in the U.S. soon after the first oil well was drilled in Titusville, Pennsylvania. He made his way to the Franklin, Titusville, Oil City area and started making barrels for oil the same way and size as he had made barrels for wine in Germany.

Barry's great grandfather's name was Peter and he married a tiny Quaker lady named Elizabeth. They gave birth to 15 babies. Only six babies lived. It was not an easy life.

In St. Wendel, I found a man who gave me names and information on the Kockler line back to 1600. There are not many Kocklers in the U.S. other than our relatives. In St. Wendel there are Kocklers everywhere. We ate at a very old restaurant owned by Kocklers. We passed a lawyer's office with the name Kockler on the door. We went to a tea shop owned by Kocklers. We saw the two houses that Peter Kockler grew up in. It was a wonderful two days.

HOWARD (MY FATHER'S FAMILY)

Barry and I visited the Castle Howard in England some years ago. I remember walking through the halls with all the Howard men's pictures that had lived there through the years. My father, Everett Howard, looked so much like all these men.

Aristocrats of England flocked to Virginia and then to the Carolinas as land became available. In England, the eldest son inherited everything leaving younger sons without land.

Alexander Howard was born in Spotsylvania, Virginia in 1700. He died in 1759 in Virginia. His son Peter Howard moved to Greenville County, SC and died there in 1810. He was the start of the Howards of Glassy Mountain, SC. He is buried in Howard Cemetery on Highway 11 beside where his son's home was. Highway 11 was built on top of the homestead.

Thomas Howard was the son of Peter Howard. He led a group from the area with an Indian friend on a raid to kill Indians who had killed several area children. There is a monument to him and

Howard Gap Road through the mountains is named for him. He became very famous in the area. Thomas was born in Greenville County, SC and died there in 1840. He is also buried in Howard Cemetery off Highway 11. He is my four times great grandfather.

The area of Greenville County that the Howards populated became known as "The Dark Corner." It was such a poor area and very remote. There were no cash crops in those mountains other than moonshine. Corn would sell for $2.50 a bushel. That bushel of corn would make enough moonshine to sell for $6.50. The area was written up in New York newspapers many times because of the murders committed there over the moonshine stills.

One Sunday morning in front of Hilltop Church on Glassy Mountain, four men got into an argument and shot each other killing two men. Two of these men were Howards. There were so many fathers getting killed that their families were starving to death. James Holland Howard who was well respected in the community called everyone together to form an alliance against moonshining. Many signed up to form this alliance and to report stills and to help revenuers close the stills. James Holland Howard who led this alliance was shot to death by moonshiners while he was leading a revenuer group into the area of a still in 1924. This outraged so many people in the area that they started trying to find new ways to earn a living. Peach trees have helped in this drive. Many people started working in knitting mills which had moved into Greenville.

The oldest son of James Holland Howard who started the alliance was in seminary to become a minister at the time of his father's death. Dr. James A. Howard became a well-known preacher and taught in the 1950s at Southwestern Baptist Theological Seminary in Fort Worth, Texas. I lived only four blocks from there in the 1950s.

I wish I could have known what I know now and could have talked to him. I was only 12 years old at the time we moved there.

Barry and I visited the "Dark Corner" recently. Rich retirement communities are now everywhere with golf courses around every corner. There are small Baptist churches about every three miles with a cemetery beside each church. We had a guide drive us on a special Howard tour. He said that three or four miles was about how far a family could go on a horse-pulled wagon to and from church. Every cemetery had lots of Howard graves. The Glassy Mountain Baptist Church Cemetery had hundreds of Howard graves back to the 1790s.

These churches are still active today. It is such a beautiful area. Our guide was a lifelong resident there and his great grandmother had been a Howard.

I believe that P.L. Howard is Pleasant Leonard Howard who moved to Gilmer, Georgia. He is the father of Anderson Howard who moved to Evening Shade, Arkansas. He married Sarah Lawhorn. They were the parents of Joseph Howard who married Martha Lankford of Evening Shade, Arkansas. They were my grandparents. They moved to Oklahoma where my father Everett Howard was born.

There is another family who descended from my dad's Uncle Will who are big into Ancestry.com. They have P.L. Howard as being Priestly Leonard Howard. They have P.L. Howard born in the county next to Greenville County, SC. It is only a few miles from Glassy Mountain. I think they would have to be from the same families, but they trace that line back to mostly Howard Castle. They may be right. These ancestors used the same names for generations. There were two Pleasant Howards who were cousins. One moved to Gilmer County, GA and one moved to Kentucky. They were both born at Glassy Mountain, SC.

Any family member who might be interested in more on this family can talk to me for more information. I can't make this book go on forever!

TALLEY (MY GRANDMA TALLEY LOYD'S FAMILY)

John Talley was born in Staffordshire, England. He died in Jamestown, VA. He came to Virginia with his wife and three sons in 1630. Six generations later, Benoni Talley was born in 1775 in Mecklenburg County, Virginia. He and his brother James Dudley came to Cocke County, Tennessee in 1795.

Most sources say the Talleys were French Huguenot who came to England to escape persecution. Benoni is the French word for Benjamin.

Benoni Talley's son Bradley W. Talley was born in 1804 in Cocke County, Tennessee and died there in 1875. Bradley W. Talley was Lannie Belle Talley's grandfather. Bradley W. Talley's son, William Buckner Jefferson Talley, was the father of my grandmother Lannie Belle.

William Buckner Jefferson Talley was born in 1849 in Cocke County, Tennessee. He married Sena Crumbley and is shown in the 1880 census in Chuckey Knobbs, Cocke County, Tennessee. Cocke County was and still is one of the poorest counties in Tennessee.

Lannie Belle Talley was born in 1886 in Cocke County, Tennessee. She was one of the younger children. I think she was about eight years old when the family moved to Jackson County, Alabama. She married Ike Loyd in 1900 in Jackson County, Alabama.

All of the Talley girls married all the Loyd boys. One Loyd girl married one Talley boy. All my mother's cousins were double cousins. I think the Loyds and Talleys were the only families on the mountain.

My grandmother told my mother that Ike had been wanting to move to Oklahoma for some years. Grandma told him she would not leave Alabama until her mother died. Sena Talley died in 1922. They moved to Oklahoma in 1927.

Ike had said he was afraid that if he stayed in Jackson County that his kids might marry a cousin. Barry and I were there working on some ancestry information. We had two of my cousins with us who grew up in the area. Their grandmother was an older sister of my mother. She had stayed and settled in Chattanooga when the family moved to Oklahoma.

Barry and I and these two cousins were looking for a cemetery. We stopped at a post office to get directions. There were three ladies in the post office. We told the three ladies we were looking for information on ancestors with the last names of Loyd, Talley, and Matthews. They all said they didn't know much about their ancestors, but one said her husband was a Matthews and her mother was a Talley.

One lady said one grandmother was a Loyd and her other grandmother was a Matthews. Her husband was a Talley. Same thing was the story of the other lady. My cousins and I laughed all the way to the car.

All three of those ladies were married to a cousin and did not know it, and they were all related to the three of us. Guess my grandfather was right. The ladies were able to give information for us to find the cemeteries. It was a fun day.

Barry and I have spent time on two different trips to Cocke County, Tennessee. It is not far from Smoky Mountain National Park. The Smoky Mountains are our favorite places on earth. Our friends, Judy and Jon Markland, were with us on our first trip. The Marklands lived in Double Oak when we first came back to Texas.

They live in Indiana now. We had met in the mountains for a week-long visit. One day, we went to Cocke County. We all have great memories from that day.

I had done a lot of research of the area and the Talleys before we were there. Talley Hollow Road is where all the census from 1840 and forward showed the Talleys living. This road runs along Chuckey Knobs River. Benoni Talley had settled on this road in the late 1700s.

We found Talley Hollow Road and found a Bobby Talley living on the corner. I got out of the car to visit with him when we saw him in the back yard of his house. I asked him how to find the old Talley cemetery, which was on the farm that Benoni settled in the late 1700s. Bobby said that "His dead was dead." Barry has a picture of my perplexed face looking at Bobby trying to figure what he was saying. Then Bobby said, "My dead knew all the family history." Then I realized he was saying his "Dad was dead"!

Bobby explained the river runs over Talley Hollow Road. We would have to enter the other end of the road to find the cemetery on Benoni's land. He told us to go up the rise (that is a hill) and turn right at a country store. We found the country store which had been closed for three years. I have since learned that two story building was built in 1917 and was the Talley Memorial Schoolhouse. We never found the cemetery which is, again, in a pasture with no sign. It cannot be seen from the road.

We have found other old cemeteries such as the Talley Cemetery in old pastures. They have been so overgrown with a hundred years of fallen trees and vines. I have not been able to walk through them but can just see the tops of tombstones. We did find the cemetery where Benoni's brother was buried. It is on the land James Dudley Talley settled. I could not walk on it but got some pictures. It had a fence to keep cows out but had not been cared for in a hundred years. I guess all the family have moved away.

I had a family reunion at my house a few months after meeting Bobby Talley. I sent him some pictures and was looking forward to seeing him again on our second trip a couple of years later. Bobby Talley had died. I think he was the last of the Talleys in the area. One family group went to Missouri. Another went to Chattanooga, Tennessee. There is a Talley Road in Chattanooga where they settled.

There was a house across the road from Bobby. It looked like a real Appalachian home with old tools in the front yard and old couches on the front porches. In the middle of this mess were a lot of flowers from the nursery waiting to be planted. I wanted to meet the lady of this house who had the spirit to plant beautiful flowers in the middle of all this junk.

Barry, of course, said, "You should not go to that door. Someone might shoot you." I went to the door. My friend Judy in the back seat told Barry that he should go to the door with me. He explained that he was going to keep the car going for us to have a quick escape. When I went to the door, I saw about 20 large, very large, mean-looking dogs in small cages and tied to trees. They were not happy about my being there and were very loud. I am sure that the people did not feed that many mean dogs for fun. The dogs served some purpose. I can only guess. I knocked on the door and a lot of dogs inside all hit the door hard and barked. No one came to the door, so I went back to the car which was full of three very scared people and we left.

The Marklands laughed so hard when I was trying to figure out what "My dead is dead" meant. The whole car was shaking. They said they loved to go on vacation with me. I make sure it is a memory filled trip. I love hearing local accents. Most of us sound too much alike. It was a joy visiting with Bobby Talley.

Talley Memorial School built in 1917 in Cocke County, Tennessee.

(Insert PJ43. Bobby Talley telling me that his dead is dead.

MATTHEWS OF JACKSON COUNTY, ALABAMA

My grandfather was a Loyd. It is not possible to trace the Loyd family. His father left and no one knows about him. Ike Loyd's mother was a Matthews. Barry and the two cousins and I on our day of exploring were out to find Matthews Cove. The two cousins had never heard of this place. The ladies in the post office told us how to find it. They delivered mail there. It is the most remote place in the most remote county in Alabama. That is what I had read doing my research before we had left home.

We started on a two-lane gravel road. It became a dirt road. Then it was a one-lane dirt trail. Mountains were almost against our car on both sides. There was a waterfall coming down against one side of the car. Barry kept wanting to turn around. I kept encouraging him to keep going. We were in a four-wheel drive rental car which was a good thing. Finally, after some time, in front of us opened up a beautiful cove surrounded by mountains. The land was perfectly flat. The mountains went straight up from the flat land. There was a pasture on the left side with one large wild cherry tree. It had a fence around it with graves inside the fence.

Barry said I could not go over the fence. I told him that the law says a landowner cannot keep people from a cemetery. He said that he was not sure anyone here would be well acquainted with the law. I told him to stay in the car and go for help if someone shot me. Weeds were higher than my knees. I was more afraid of snakes than being shot. We yelled out and knocked on the house door. No one was there but two men came out of the chicken house. They didn't speak much English but told us to go.

There were two tombstones and many rocks and stones that could not be read. This family was here in this cove long before the Indians were moved out! White men were not allowed to live in this area before the Indian removal. Maybe the Indians could not find them and did not know they were there. Or maybe they let them stay for the moonshine.

Ike Loyd's grandfather was big into moonshine. His nickname was "Puncheon" (French for maker of spirits). He was James "Puncheon" Jim Matthews. He was in jail for moonshining around 1850. After that, he bought some land further up the mountain making it harder for the law to find. This land had a freshwater spring on it. I wonder if the waterfall which fell on us is from that spring.

Walker Matthews came to Jackson County, Alabama in early 1800s. He either came from Savannah, Georgia or from Kentucky. Walker was the father of Jim "Puncheon" Matthews. Jim's daughter was Sarah Matthews who was Ike Loyd's mother.

I read that the Matthews in Matthews Cove raised some of the best horses in the county. They sold moonshine and horses. My grandfather said he started helping his grandfather in the still when he was nine years old.

My grandfather never went to school and could not read when he married my grandmother. My grandmother taught him to read. He was not educated but was a smart man in so many ways.

LANKFORD AND FERGUSON

My father's grandmother was Margaret Ferguson Lankford. Margaret's father was John Harvey Ferguson. He was born in North Carolina. Everett's great great grandfather was born in 1700 in Scotland. His great grandfather was born in Northern Ireland in 1724.

England would give land in Ireland to people in Scotland. This was done to make Ireland into a Protestant nation. Scotland was Protestant. Ireland was Catholic. England wanted to make Ireland a Protestant nation. This is where we get the expression of Scott's Irish. This is what led to the problems in Ireland between the Protestants and Catholics.

John Harvey Ferguson's great great grandfather and great grandfather came to Crowders Creek, North Carolina in 1750. John Harvey Ferguson's father was born in North Carolina and died in North Carolina. John Harvey Ferguson was born in North Carolina in 1821. John moved to Izard County, Arkansas where Martha Ferguson Lankford was born. Martha, Everett Howard's mother, was born in Izard County, Arkansas. She married Joseph Howard.

John Harvey Ferguson moved to Denton County, Texas later in life. He is buried in Eakin Cemetery close to Ponder, Texas. My family had a picnic there and worked on the damaged tombstone.

LANKFORD

Arthur Lankford appears in 1830 census records of Lawrence County, Arkansas. Lawrence County became Izard County. Arthur Lankford received a land grant because he served in the War of 1812. Arthur was my dad's great great grandfather. Parks Lankford was the son of Arthur. Parks met his future wife Thursey at an old time camp meeting near Zion, Arkansas. These camp meetings lasted a week. People would bring their cows so they could be milked regularly and would bring the dogs also.

Parks and Thursey were the parents of Henry Lankford. Henry and Margaret Lankford were the parents of Martha Lankford. Martha married Joseph Howard. They were my father Everett Howard's parents. My dad's parents left Arkansas and moved, along with Martha's two sisters, to Oklahoma. Henry and Margaret Langford were married for over 75 years.

www.ingramcontent.com/pod-product-compliance
Lightning Source LLC
Chambersburg PA
CBHW060527100426
42743CB00009B/1447